Learning About Books & Libraries

A Gold Mine of Games

Carol K. Lee & Janet Langford

Alleyside Press

Fort Atkinson, Wisconsin

Additional Books by Carol K. Lee

57 Games to Play in the Library or Classroom
Carol Lee and Fay Edwards (1-57950-014-5)

Storytime Companion: Learning Games & Activities for Schools & Libraries Carol Lee and Janet Langford (1-57950-019-6)

Published by Alleyside Press
An imprint of Highsmith Press LLC
W5527 Highway 106
P.O. Box 800
Fort Atkinson, Wisconsin 53538-0800
1-800-558-2110

Library of Congress Cataloging-in-Publication Data

Lee, Carol K.
 Learning about books & libraries: a gold mine of games /
Carol K. Lee and Janet Langford.
 p. cm.
 Includes bibliographical references and index.
 ISBN 1-57950-51-X (soft : alk. paper)
 1. Library orientation for school children–United States.
2. Elementary school libraries–United States–Problems, exercises, etc. 3. Educational games–United States. 4. Library orientation for school children. 5. Elementary school libraries–Problems, exercises, etc. 6. Educational games. I. Title: Learning about books and libraries. II. Langford, Janet. III. Title.

Z711.2.L455 2000
027.62'5–dc21   00-029288

Contents

Introduction

Learning about Books and Libraries follows the same format of the popular *57 Games to Play in the Library or Classroom*. Grade-level recommendations are at the top of each game description and in the index. Most of the games may be played with at least three grade levels, depending on the difficulty of the questions, the skill taught, or the literature-based books used with the games.

Making and Playing the Games

Examples of the game boards, patterns, and sample questions have been provided to expedite the preparation of the games. We have estimated number of minutes required to make each game if you are using the patterns and questions provided. Most of the games do not take more than thirty minutes to make.

While many of the games may be drawn on the chalkboard, directions for making a permanent game board are given because it is our experience that most teachers prefer to create something they can use again and again.

When making or selecting game markers, it's important to choose items that can be easily seen by the entire class. We suggest clips, clamps, or clothespins because these are easy to move around the edges of the board. They may be purchased from a grocery store, hardware store, or a discount store. Post-It note paper or double-stick tape may be used with game pieces to mark the moves that are away from the edges of the poster board. The note paper or tape will need to be replaced after each game.

While all the games are designed to be used with the entire class, they certainly may be used with smaller groups. The directions also suggest when certain games are best played with more than two teams, sometimes up to four teams.

Some games require students to do preliminary research in their teams. The directions for each game state whether teams should select a group recorder or use individual chalkboards to give their answers when the game is played.

Some directions recommend a time limit for doing group work. The students are directed to divide the responsibilities of the research task and to share their findings with the other members of the team.

The average time for actually playing the games should not be more than 30 minutes. A short review of the particular skill the game is related to and a brief introduction to the game and the rules should precede each game.

How to Use This Book

The games here are intended as a follow up to lessons on certain skills, not to introduce or teach these skills. They are designed to enhance the lessons, to review, or to serve as an activity following a particular story.

The first group of games relates to fiction books. We have selected only fiction titles that are currently in print. Other similar books not in print may still be in your library, and you may adapt games to those books. We have suggested books that we feel are likely to be found in most school library collections.

The "fiction" games relate to review of plots, characters, settings, authors, and Newbery and Caldecott Medal winners. Again, most of the games may be played on any grade level depending on the difficulty of the questions you devise and the books used with the games.

The next group of games pertain to nonfiction books, recognition of Dewey Decimal numbers, map skills, and research resources, including electronic sources.

Several games require the use of computers to retrieve information. We have not suggested as many websites as titles of books, as sites change frequently.

A few games related to the biography section follow next. An introduction to the biography section is usually made to students at about the second-grade level and continues to the fourth grade.

An assortment of games that can be used with thematic units or to follow up a particular book are in the last section. We realize that while we have suggested specific book titles to you, we may have excluded books that work better or as well as the ones we've chosen. The books listed are the ones we currently are familiar with. Feel free to use books that you know, enjoy, or that have just arrived in your library.

We have made an effort not to reuse certain games, such as BINGO or matching games. Rather we have tried to provide a variety of types of games—board games, active games, research-related games, etc. Game ideas for one skill can easily be adapted for another skill.

The index provides information on the grade and curricular skills for which the games are intended.

Combining this book with *57 Games to Play in the Library or Classroom* you have more than one hundred game ideas to make learning about the library and the use of books fun. The books and games selected here complement the ideas found in *Storytime Companion*, providing you with a wealth of activities to promote the love of books. We hope your students will treasure the fun experiences you provide as a result of the ideas we have presented.

Book Clues

Purpose

To review fiction books.

To Make

Write clues related to a select number of fiction books on index cards, five clues per book. Each card relates to one book. See the examples provided below and on the next page.

🕰 Preparation time—30 minutes.

To Play

Start the game by having a team member from one team draw an index card and hand it to you. Read the first clue. The team may ask for a second clue. At any point the team may decide to state the title of the book the clues relate to.

If the response is correct, the team earns the number of points equal to the number of clues you *didn't* give. If incorrect the team does not get any points for that round.

The game continues with the other team following the same procedure. The game ends when all cards have been drawn or at a designated time period. The team with the most points wins the game.

Clue 1
   Folklore.

Clue 2
   Main character is female.

Clue 3
   Winner of the 1998 Caldecott Medal.

Clue 4
   For stealing a certain plant, her parents had to give her to a sorceress.

Clue 5
   She was locked in a tower, but rescued by a prince.

Answer: *Rapunzel*

Rapunzel by Paul O. Zelinsky. Scholastic, 1997.

Sample Books with Clues

Book 1

Clue 1 Animal story.

Clue 2 Main character does not enjoy eating bugs.

Clue 3 She lives with a bird family although she is not a bird.

Clue 4 She is happily reunited with her mother.

Clue 5 She is a fruit bat.

Answer: Stellaluna [by Janelle Cannon. Scholastic, 1993.]

Book 2

Clue 1 Caldecott Honor Book.

Clue 2 The setting is Italy.

Clue 3 Two main characters are a witch and her helper.

Clue 4 The witch warns her helper not to touch her pasta pot.

Clue 5 Pasta flows from the pot and threatens to cover the town.

Answer: Strega Nona [by Tomie de Paola. Simon & Schuster, 1975.]

Book 3

Clue 1 Picture book.

Clue 2 The setting is Paris, France.

Clue 3 The main character lives with eleven other girls.

Clue 4 The main character has her appendix removed.

Clue 5 Miss Clavel, a nun, takes care of the girls.

Answer: Madeline [by Ludwig Bemelmans. Scholastic, 1982.]

Book 4

Clue 1 An easy fiction book.

Clue 2 The character's crime appears in a newspaper.

Clue 3 He wanted to bake a cake for his "dear old granny."

Clue 4 His cold caused the crimes to be committed.

Clue 5 He was put in jail for his crimes.

Answer: The True Story of the 3 Little Pigs [by Jon Scieszka. Puffin, 1989.]

Book 5

Clue 1 A folktale.

Clue 2 The story takes place on a cold winter day.

Clue 3 A boy loses something.

Clue 4 Various animals seek a warm place in the boy's lost item.

Clue 5 The lost item is a mitten.

Answer: The Mitten [by Jan Brett. Scholastic, 1989.]

Book 6

Clue 1 A folktale.

Clue 2 The characters are animals.

Clue 3 One character is lazy. The other character outsmarts him.

Clue 4 Vegetables are grown in the story.

Clue 5 The hare family motivates the bear to plant his own garden.

Answer: Tops & Bottoms [by Janet Stevens. Scholastic, 1995.]

Name That Book!

Purpose

To have students read and write summaries of fiction books.

To promote interest in fiction books.

To Make

Have each child read a fiction book, write a summary of the plot on index cards (larger cards for younger children), and read their summaries to the entire class. Explain that the summaries will be used for a game so the title should not be mentioned in the written summary. However the title is stated in the oral report.

⏰ Preparation time—Depends on whether the books are easy fiction or novel length. Reading easy fiction books and reporting on them may take anywhere from one to two hours. Intermediate-level books may take several weeks.

You will need a timer for this activity.

To Play

Divide the class into two teams. Collect the cards and divide into two sets. Each team receives the cards written by the members of the other team.

Decide which team will be first. Explain that the team has 60 seconds to determine what book the summary is about. Take a card from the stack of cards written by the opposite team. At the click of the timer, start reading the summary. The team may say "Stop!" at any point, and the timer is stopped.

The team announces the title of the book. If it's correct, the number of seconds is subtracted from the 60-seconds of allotted time. The remainder is what the team earns for that round. If incorrect, the team scores no points for that round.

Continue the same procedure with the other team. The team with the most points wins the game.

Grades 1–4

Musical Fiction Bag Drop

Purpose

To review elements related to fiction books.

To Make

Use the pattern on the next page to make a game cube. Enlarge the pattern on a copier to make a larger cube (if desired). A 2" wooden block may be purchased from a craft store and used instead. Use a marker to write the words on the block.

You will need a paper bag and tapes with music for this activity. Each student will need to have read a fiction book and have the book on hand.

⏰ Preparation time—30 minutes.

To Play

Divide the group into two or more teams. Show students the terms on the game cube and give examples of responses for each word (see suggestions below). Place the cube in the paper bag. Have the students put their fiction books on their desks.

Start the music. The students pass the paper bag to each other in the order you designate. Stop the music intermittently. Direct the student holding the bag when the music stops to take the cube out of the bag and read the word of the top side of the cube. The student then relates the word to the appropriate information of his/her book.

If correct, the student earns a point for his/her team. The student places the cube into the bag and the game continues as the music resumes. The team with the most points wins the game.

Review the Terms Used on the Game Cube

Genre: Give examples of types of book genres: mystery, animal story, chapter book, friendship, historical fiction

Illustration: Art media used by the illustrator; (chalk; paint; collage)

Characters: Personality and physical description of main characters

Title Page: Point to the information on that appears on the title page and explain what it represents.

Setting: Explain where the story takes place; also may relate setting to a particular time period if story takes place in a different time

Plot: Summary of the story

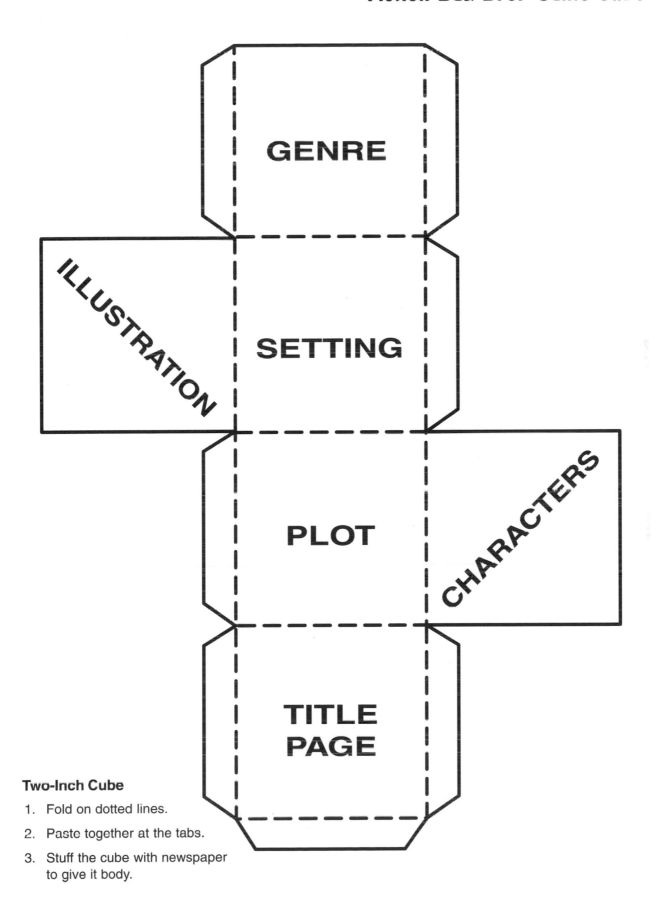

GENRE

ILLUSTRATION

SETTING

PLOT

CHARACTERS

TITLE PAGE

Two-Inch Cube

1. Fold on dotted lines.

2. Paste together at the tabs.

3. Stuff the cube with newspaper to give it body.

Bean Bag Book Toss

Purpose

To review plots of fiction books in sequence.

To Make

Make or buy a bean bag.

Using masking tape, mark an "X" on the floor to designate a "toss" area from which a player tosses the beanbag.

⏰ Preparation time—30 minutes.

To Play

Read six fiction books to your students (appropriate to their age group) over a period of time. Write the titles on cards.

Divide the class into two teams. The class members may remain seated at their desks. Have the first player of one team stand in the "toss" area and pick a card.

Direct the player to toss the bean bag to a player on his/her team. The other team members may not try to catch the bag. If a team member successfully catches the bag, that player starts telling the plot of the story indicated on the card. That player should not tell more than one event in the story.

That player then goes to the "toss" area to continue the same procedure. The person who catches the bag continues by telling the next action in the story. The round ends when the team members complete the story. The team earns one point for each person's retelling of the story in the correct sequence of events. No points are given for "backtracking" of the plot from the previous retelling.

The game continues with the other team. When all cards have been drawn, the team with the most points is declared the winner.

Book Character Scramble

Purpose

To review favorite picture book characters.

To Make

Measure and mark every two inches, horizontally and vertically, on a 22" X 28" (standard size) poster board. Draw a grid-like pattern as shown in the example. Shade about three squares in the center area to designate a starting point. Designate bonus squares. Laminate the board.

Make two copies of page 14. Cut the letter pieces into 2" squares. Put the letters in a paper bag.

Duplicate the list of book characters, one list per team, and give to each team.

🕐 Preparation time—30 minutes

To Play

Divide the class into three to four teams. Direct a player from each team to pull ten letters from the paper bag.

Have a player from one team give you the letters to form the name of one book character and tell you where to place the name on the board. Write the character's name, horizontally or vertically as stated by the team, on the board with a washable marker. Add the points on the letter squares. Double the total points if any letter square is placed on a bonus square. Use the bonus square only once. Put the letter squares aside and have the player take more letters (number of letters used) to have ten in all.

Continue with the other team. Each time have the player tell where the character's name will connect to the letters. If a team cannot form a character's name, the team receives no points but may exchange three letters from the bag.

The game ends when no team can form book characters' names. The team with the most points wins the game.

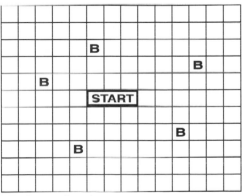

sample game board

Book Character Scramble Letters

A 1	A 1	A 1	A 1	A 1	A 1	A 1	B 3
C 2	C 2	C 2	C 2	D 2	D 2	D 2	E 1
E 1	E 1	E 1	E 1	E 1	E 1	F 2	F 2
F 2	G 2	G 2	G 2	G 2	H 3	H 3	I 1
I 1	I 1	I 1	I 1	I 1	J 3	K 3	K 3
L 2	L 2	L 2	L 2	M 2	M 2	M 2	N 2
N 2	N 2	O 1	O 1	O 1	O 1	O 1	P 3
Q 3	R 1	R 1	R 1	R 1	R 1	R 1	S 2
S 2	S 2	T 2	T 2	T 2	U 1	U 1	U 1
U 1	V 3	W 3	W 3	X 3	Y 3	Y 3	Z 3
0	0	0	0	0	0	0	0

Book Character Scramble

1. ANANSI (spider)

2. ANGUS (*Angus and the Cat; Angus and the Ducks; Angus Lost*)

3. ARTHUR (aardvark)

4. BOA (*The Day Jimmy's Boa Ate the Wash*)

5. CLIFFORD (big red dog)

6. CORDUROY (*Corduroy; A Pocket for Corduroy*)

7. DRAGON (*A Friend for Dragon; Dragon's Halloween*)

8. D.W. (*D.W. Thinks Big; D.W., Go to Your Room!; D.W. Rides Again; D.W. the Picky Eater* and more)

9. FRANKLIN (turtle)

10. GEORGE (*Curious George*; also George and Martha books)

11. GEORGIE (ghost)

12. GRACE (*Amazing Grace*)

13. HARRY (*Harry the Dirty Dog; No Roses for Harry; Harry by the Sea*)

14. JACK (*Jack and the Beanstalk*)

15. LISA (*Corduroy; A Pocket for Corduroy*)

16. MADELINE (*Madeline; Madeline's Rescue*)

17. MAX (*Where the Wild Things Are; Max's Dragon Shirt*)

18. MCDUFF (*McDuff Moves In; McDuff Comes Home; McDuff and the Baby*)

19. PETER (*Peter's Chair; A Snowy Day; Whistle for Willie*)

20. SAL (*Blueberries for Sal*)

21. SWIMMY (fish)

22. TROLL (*Trouble With Troll; The Three Billy Goats Gruff*)

Grades 3–5

Fiction Charades

Purpose

To have fun with fiction titles

To Make

Prepare and duplicate a list of popular fiction books for each team. Make sure to select titles that have words for which students can provide nonverbal clues. In addition to the list, write each title on a card, one title per card.

You will need a timer.

⏰ Preparation time—15 minutes

To Play

Divide the class into three teams. Direct each team to select several "actors." During each team's turn, one actor draws a title card. The actors start providing nonverbal clues (pantomime) at the "go" signal to their other team members. The timer is clicked on.

The non-acting team members may blurt out individual words from a title. If they say the entire title, the timer is stopped. The time is recorded if the title is correct. If not, the team is disqualified for that round.

Follow the same procedure for the other teams. The team with the least number of minutes wins that round. The game may continue with a second and third round. The team that wins the most rounds wins the game.

Sample Titles

The Cat in the Hat	*Rabbit Hill*
Charlotte's Web	*Sign of the Beaver*
Chocolate Fever	*Skinnybones*
Dear Mr. Henshaw	*A Taste of Blackberries*
Encyclopedia Brown	*The Velveteen Rabbit*
Freckle Juice	*The Lion, the Witch, and the Wardrobe*
Hatchet	*The Hundred Dresses*
The Indian in the Cupboard	*Island of the Blue Dolphins*
The Whipping Boy	*The Mouse and the Motorcycle*

Newbery Clues

Purpose

To review Newbery Medal books.

To Make

Copy the list of Newbery Medal winners, one for each student.

Current lists of the Newbery Medal winners as well as the Caldecott winners may be found at the American Library Association website (**www.ala.org/alsc/newbpast.html**) Additional award lists for children's literature can be found at the Children's Literature Web Guide (**www.ucalgary.ca/~dkbrown/index.html**).

Use the sample clues to play this game. You will need five individual chalkboards, five erasers, and five pieces of chalk for this game.

⏰ Preparation time—15 minutes

To Play

Divide the class into five teams. Give the list of Newbery Medal winners to each student. Have each team select a recorder. Ask two students to serve as referees. Tell them they must watch and listen closely because they will be deciding which team completes the activities first.

When a clue is given to the entire class, the teams tell their recorders to write their answers. To find the answer, the team must locate the book in the clue, and then write down the _year_ that book won the award. Sometimes the answer may include more than one year.

When the recorder has completed writing on the board, he/she yells, "Done!" The referees decide who was first. If the answer is correct, the team earns a point. Optional: More points may be earned if the clue has multiple answers.

If the answer is incorrect, no point is given for that clue.

The team with the most points wins the game.

Newbery Clues

1. The donor (*The Giver,* 1994)

2. A Civil War battlefield (*Shiloh,* 1992)

3. Punishment for a bad kid (*The Whipping Boy,* 1987)

4. Title has name of a sea mammal (*Island of the Blue Dolphins,* 1961)

5. Title has name of a mountain range in South America (*Secret of the Andes,* 1953)

6. Royal person mentioned three times (*King of the Wind,* 1949; *The Grey King,* 1976; *The High King,* 1969)

7. A number besides two (*The Twenty-One Balloons,* 1948)

8. An adult male deer (*The White Stag,* 1938)

9. A pioneer explorer (*Daniel Boone,* 1940)

10. Title has name of a vegetable (*Onion John,* 1960)

11. Weapons in the title (*Rifles for Watie,* 1958; *The Bronze Bow,* 1962; *The Matchlock Gun,* 1942)

12. Crazy person (*Maniac Magee,* 1991)

13. Title has the name of a fruit (*Strawberry Girl,* 1946)

14. Title has words related to the weather (*King of the Wind,* 1949; *Roll of Thunder, Hear My Cry,* 1977)

15. An American president (*Lincoln : A Photobiography,* 1988)

16. Bodies of water (*Witch of Blackbird Pond,* 1959; *Shen of the Sea,* 1926)

17. A month (*Missing May,* 1993)

18. A season (*Thimble Summer,* 1939; *Summer of the Swans,* 1971)

19. Day of the week (*The View from Saturday,* 1997)

20. Title has a color word (*Island of the Blue Dolphins,* 1961; *The Grey King,* 1976)

21. Two things in space (*Walk Two Moons,* 1995; *Number the Stars,* 1990)

22. A spice (*Ginger Pye,* 1952)

23. Three names starting with a "J" (*Jacob Have I Loved,* 1981; *Onion John,* 1960; *Julie of the Wolves,*1973; *I, Juan de Pareja,* 1966; *Johnny Tremain,*1944)

24. A medical title (*Voyages of Doctor Dolittle,* 1923)

25. A male cow (*Shadow of a Bull,* 1965)

Newbery Medal Books

2000 ***Bud, Not Buddy*** **(Christopher Paul Curtis)**

1999 *Holes* (Louis Sachar)

1998 *Out of the Dust* (Karen Hesse)

1997 *The View From Saturday* (E.L. Konigsburg)

1996 *The Midwife's Apprentice* (Karen Cushman)

1995 *Walk Two Moons* (Sharon Creech)

1994 *The Giver* (Lois Lowery)

1993 *Missing May* (Cynthia Rylant)

1992 *Shiloh* (Phyllis Reynolds Naylor)

1991 *Maniac Magee* (Jerry Spinelli)

1990 ***Number the Stars*** **(Lois Lowery)**

1989 *Joyful Noise:Poems for Two Voices* (Paul Fleischman)

1988 *Lincoln, A Photobiography* (Russell Freedman)

1987 *The Whipping Boy* (Sid Fleischman)

1986 *Sarah Plain and Tall* (Patricia MacLachlan)

1985 *The Hero and the Crown* (Jean Lee Latham)

1984 *Dear Mr. Henshaw* (Beverly Cleary)

1983 *Dicey's Song* (Cynthia Voigt)

1982 *A Visit to William Blake's Inn: Poems for Innocent and Experienced Travelers* (Nancy Willard)

1981 *Jacob Have I Loved* (Katherine Paterson)

1980 ***A Gathering of Days*** **(Joan W. Blos)**

1979 *The Westing Game* (Ellen Raskin)

1978 *Bridge to Terabithia* (Katherine Paterson)

1977 *Roll of Thunder, Hear My Cry* (Mildred D. Taylor)

1976 *The Grey King* (Susan Cooper)

1975 *M.C.Higgins, The Great* (Virginia Hamilton)

1974 *The Slave Dancer* (Paula Fox)

1973 *Julie of the Wolves* (Jean Craighead George)

1972 *Mrs. Frisby and the Rats of NIMH* (Robert C. O'Brien)

1971 *Summer of the Swans* (Betsy Byars)

1970 ***Sounder*** **(William H. Armstrong)**

1969 *The High King* (Lloyd Alexander)

1968 *From the Mixed-Up Files of Mrs. Basil E. Frankweiler* (E.L. Konigsburg)

1967 *Up a Road Slowly* (Irene Hunt)

1966 *I, Juan de Pareja* (Elizabeth de Trevino)

1965 *Shadow of a Bull* (Maia Wojciechowska)

1964 *It's Like This, Cat* (Emily Neville)

1963 *A Wrinkle in Time* (Madeline L'Engle)

1962 *The Bronze Bow* (Elizabeth Speare)

1961 *Island of the Blue Dolphins* (Scott O'Dell)

1960 *Onion John* (Joseph Krumgold)

1959 *The Witch of Blackbird Pond* (Elizabeth Speare)

1958 *Rifles for Watie* (Harold Keith)

1957 *Miracles on Maple Hill* (Virginia Sorenson)

1956 *Carry on, Mr. Bowditch* (Robin McKinley)

1955 *The Wheel on the School* (Meindert De Jong)

1954 *And Now Miguel* (Joseph Krumgold)

1953 *Secret of the Andes* (Ann Nolan Clark)

1952 *Ginger Pye* (Eleanor Estes)

1951 *Amos Fortune, Free Man* (Elizabeth Yates)

1950 *The Door in the Wall* (Marguerite de Angeli)

1949 *King of the Wind* (Marguerite Henry)

1948 *The Twenty-One Balloons* (William du Bois)

1947 *Miss Hickory* (Carolyn Bailey)

1946 *Strawberry Girl* (Lois Lenski)

1945 *Rabbit Hill* (Robert Lawson)

1944 *Johnny Tremain* (Esther Forbes)

1943 *Adam of the Road* (Elizabeth Gray)

1942 *The Matchlock Gun* (Walter D. Edmonds)

1941 *Call It Courage* (Armstrong Sperry)

1940 *Daniel Boone* (James Daugherty)

1939 *Thimble Summer* (Elizabeth Enright)

1938 *The White Stag* (Kate Seredy)

1937 *Roller Skates* (Ruth Sawyer)

1936 *Caddie Woodlawn* (Carol R. Brink)

1935 *Dobry* (Monica Shannon)

1934 *Invincible Louisa* (Cornelia Meigs)

1933 *Young Fu of the Upper Yangtze* (Elizabeth Lewis)

1932 *Waterless Mountain* (Laura Adams Armer)

1931 *The Cat Who Went to Heaven* (Elizabeth Coatsworth)

1930 *Hitty, Her First Hundred Years* (Rachel Field)

1929 *The Trumpeter of Krakow* (Eric P. Kelly)

1928 *Gay-Neck* (Dhan Gopal Mukerji)

1927 *Smoky, the Cowhorse* (Will James)

1926 *Shen of the Sea* (Arthur Chrisman)

1925 *Tales from Silver Lands* (Charles J. Finger)

1924 *The Dark Frigate* (Charles Hawes)

1923 *The Voyages of Doctor Dolittle* (Hugh Lofting)

1922 *The Story of Mankind* (Hendrik Van Loon)

Who's the Author?

Purpose

To acquaint students with well-known authors and the books they've written.

To Make

Print the names of five authors on 3" X 5" index cards, one name per card. Print five sets of cards with each set having each author's name. Color-code each set for convenience in keeping the sets together. Tape a small piece of Velcro behind each card.

Tape two poster boards together to make a large game board. List the titles of some of the books of the five authors. Write about thirteen titles of books on one side of the poster board (26 on both sides). Tape a small piece of Velcro beside each title as shown in the example.

⏰ Preparation time—40 minutes

Approximate time to introduce authors: 2 weeks

To Play

Acquaint the students with the five authors by reading books written by these authors. Follow-up with discussion of character development, style of illustration, comparison between the authors, and information about the authors' lives. **Select authors appropriate for your students' reading level.**

Divide the class into five teams. Place a set of cards, face down, on each team's table. Designate a person on each team as the "starter." Thereafter, rotate, giving each child an opportunity to draw a card.

The starter on the first team draws an author card and has fifteen seconds to decide where to put that card on the game board. He/she must place the card on the Velcro beside one of the books that author wrote. If the answer is correct, that card is left on the game board. If not, the card is placed at the bottom of the team's card stack to be drawn again.

Continue the same procedure with the other teams. The first team to place all its cards on the game board is the winner.

Who's the Author?

1. **Rainbow Fish** [Velcro]

2. **The Cat in the Hat** [Velcro]

3. **Corduroy** [Velcro]

4. **Inch by Inch** [Leo Lionni]

5. **Very Quiet Cricket** [Eric Carle]

6. **Frederick** [Velcro]

7. **Green Eggs and Ham** [Velcro]

8. **Dandelion** [Velcro]

Sample Authors

Eric Carle

Very Busy Spider. Philomel, 1984.

Very Grouchy Ladybug. HarperCollins, 1977.

Very Hungry Caterpillar. Philomel, 1969.

Very Lonely Firefly. Philomel, 1995.

Very Quiet Cricket. Philomel, 1990.

Don Freeman

Corduroy. Viking, 1968.

Dandelion. Viking, 1964.

Guard Mouse. Viking, 1967.

Mop Top. Viking, 1955.

A Pocket for Corduroy. Viking, 1978.

Ezra Jack Keats

Goggles. Macmillan, 1969.

A Letter to Amy. Harper & Row, 1968.

Peter's Chair. Harper & Row, 1967.

The Snowy Day. Viking Penguin, 1962.

Whistle for Willie. Viking Penguin, 1964.

Leo Lionni

Alexander and the Wind-Up Mouse. Pantheon, 1969.

Inch by Inch. Astor-Honor, 1960.

Fish Is Fish. Scholastic, 1970.

Frederick. Pantheon, 1967.

Swimmy. Pantheon, 1968.

Dr. Seuss

The Cat in the Hat. Random House, 1957.

Green Eggs and Ham. Random House, 1960.

Horton Hatches the Egg. Random House, 1957.

How the Grinch Stole Christmas. Random House, 1957.

One Fish, Two Fish, Red Fish, Blue Fish. Beginner Books, 1960.

Four in a Row

Purpose

To review fiction books.

To Make

Make a copy of the score sheet on the next page for each team. Create questions related to the topics listed at the top of the score sheet. The level of difficulty of the questions depends on the grade level of the students. Some sample questions for grades 3 through 5 are provided.

⏰ Preparation time—35 minutes

To Play

Divide the class into either two or four teams. Have the team members select a recorder for their team. Designate which teams will use the X and O symbols as markers.

Only two teams will play at each turn. Decide which two teams will play against each other.

Start the game by directing the first team to pick one of the topics listed on the score sheet. Ask a question related to that topic. The team decides on an answer, which is called out by the recorder. If the answer is correct, the team decides where the group's mark is to be placed in the column for that topic (i.e., Setting: 1, 5, 9, or 13).

The other team follows the same procedure. The object of the game is for the teams to get their Xs or Os aligned four in a row, across or down, or diagonally through center. They also try to prevent the other team from getting four in a row. The first team to get four in a row wins the game.

If you have four teams instead of two, have the second two teams play a round after the first game is completed. if time allows, have a third competition between the winners of the first two rounds.

Four in a Row Score Sheet

SETTING	CHARACTER	PLOT	AUTHOR or ILLUSTRATOR
1	2	3	4
5	6	7	8
9	10	11	12
13	14	15	16

Learning about Books & Libraries

Setting

1. Mr. and Mrs. Mallard found a safe home for their ducklings on an island in what city?
   a. Chicago   b. Boston   c. New York   (b)
2. What dog's new home at number 7 Elm Road smelled of sausages and vanilla rice pudding?   (McDuff)
3. Where do *A Story, A Story* and *Ashanti to Zulu* take place?   (Africa)
4. Pasta from Strega Nona's pot threatened to cover a town in _____.   (Italy)
5. In what country does the story of Lon Po Po take place?   (China)

Character

1. The characters who climbed up the coconut tree were not people or animals. What were they?   (letters)
2. When this character fell into the well, rescue was delayed all because of this long, long name. What is this character's name?   (Tikki Tikki Tembo)
3. What characters took the peddler's cap while he slept?   (monkeys)
4. Who had a terrible, no good, very bad day?   (Alexander)
5. Whose pet boa caused an uproar on a field trip to a farm?   (Jimmy)
6. What animal is Verdi?   (python)

Plot

1. In what book does Miss Viola Swamp terrify a misbehaving class?
   (Miss Nelson Is Missing)
2. In what book does food, instead of rain, fall down from the sky?
   (Cloudy with a Chance of Meatballs)
3. What happens in *The Napping House* when a flea bites a mouse?
   (everyone awakens)
4. In what story does the character, who is a housekeeper, draw a picture of drapes, hang light bulbs on clotheslines, and dress a chicken?   *(Amelia Bedelia)*
5. In what story does a family eat breakfast in the shower and mow the rug?
   (The Stupids Die)
6. In what story does the character have a scary adventure in Mr. MacGregor's garden?
   (The Tale of Peter Rabbit)

Author/Illustrator

1. David Wiesner won the Caldecott Medal for what book about frogs gliding on lily pads?   *(Tuesday)*
2. True or False? Dr. Seuss never won the Caldecott Medal.   (true)
3. What Caldecott Medal book, written by Chris Van Allsburg, is about a boxed game?
   (Jumanji)
4. Name a book, written by Ezra Jack Keats, that has a character named Peter in it.
   (Whistle for Willie; Peter's Chair; Goggles; The Snowy Day)
5. Chris Van Allsburg won the Caldecott Medal for a book about a special train. What book is it?   *(Polar Express)*
6. What type of writing is Shel Silverstein noted for?   (poetry)

Genres

Purpose

To reinforce the concept that books belong to certain genres.

To Make

Draw a circle or cut a large circle out of poster board. Divide the circle into eight pie-shaped segments. Write the following words, one in each segment:

> Mystery; Animal Story; Nonfiction; Biography; Newbery Award Winner; Caldecott Award Winner; Poetry; Folklore

Use a nail or screwdriver to bore a hole in the center of the circle. Make an arrow and fasten it with a nut and bolt in the hole.

Prepare a list of books that the students may recognize. A sample list follows this page. Duplicate the list for each team.

⏰ Preparation time—30 minutes

To Play

Divide the class into two or more teams. Have the teams designate a team member to spin for the team. When that person spins the arrow, the team has to give the title of a book from the list that belongs to the genre where the arrow stopped. Some books may belong to several genres. If so, the team may state this and receive bonus points.

Teams receive one point for each correct response. The team with the most points wins the game.

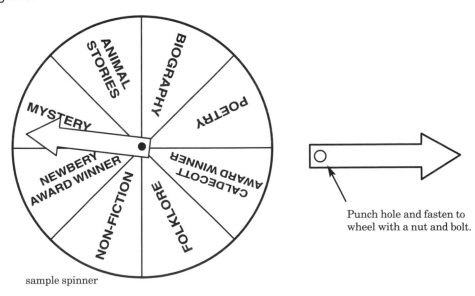

sample spinner

Punch hole and fasten to wheel with a nut and bolt.

Genre Book List

1. *Abe Lincoln's Hat* by Martha Brenner. Random House, 1994.
2. *Arthur's Eyes* by Marc Brown. Little, Brown, 1979.
3. *Bridge to Terabithia* by Katherine Paterson. Crowell, 1978.
4. *A Case for Jenny Archer* by Ellen Conford. Little, Brown, 1988.
5. *Charlotte's Web* by E. B. White. Harper Trophy, 1980.
6. *Curious George* by H. A. Rey. Houghton Mifflin, 1941.
7. *Dear Mr. Henshaw* by Beverly Cleary. Morrow, 1984.
8. *Destination Jupiter* by Seymour Simon. Morrow, 1998.
9. *Encyclopedia Brown, Boy Detective*. Lodestar, 1963.
10. *Horses* by Dorothy Hinshaw Patent. Carolrhoda, 1994.
11. *Island of the Blue Dolphins*. Houghton Mifflin, 1961.
12. *James and the Giant Peach* by Roald Dahl. Bantam, 1961.
13. *Jumanji* by Chris Van Allsburg. Houghton, 1982.
14. *The Legend of the Bluebonnet* by Tomie de Paola. Putnam, 1983.
15. *Lon Po Po* by Ed Young. Philomel, 1990.
16. *Max's Dragon Shirt* by Rosemary Wells. Dial, 1991.
17. *Minty: A Story of Young Harriet Tubman* by Alan Schroeder. Dial, 1996.
18. *My Science Book of Weather* by Neil Ardley. Harcourt Brace Jovanovich, 1992.
19. *Nate the Great* by Marjorie Weinman Sharmat. Coward, McCann, 1972.
20. *The Night Before Christmas* by Clement C. Moore. Knopf, 1990.
21. *On the Mayflower* by Kate Waters. Scholastic, 1996.
22. *Pecos Bill* by Steven Kellogg. Morrow, 1986.
23. *A Picture Book of Paul Revere* by David Adler. Holiday House, 1995.
24. *Polar Express* by Chris Van Allsburg. Houghton, 1986.
25. *Ramona the Pest* by Beverly Cleary. Dell, 1968.
26. *Read-Aloud Rhymes for the Very Young* by Jack Prelutsky. Knopf, 1986.
27. *Rumpelstiltskin* by Paul O. Zelinsky. Dutton, 1986.
28. *The Popcorn Book* by Tomie de Paola. Holiday House, 1978.
29. *Sarah Plain and Tall* by Patricia MacLachlan. Harper, 1986.
30. *Sebastian (Super Sleuth) and the Impossible Crime* by Mary Blount Christian. Macmillan, 1992.
31. *Shiloh* by Phyllis Reynolds Naylor. Atheneum, 1992.
32. *Stellaluna* by Janell Cannon. Harcourt Brace, 1993.
34. *The Three Little Pigs* by James Marshall. Dial, 1989.
35. *A Toad for Tuesday* by Russell E. Erickson. Lothrop, Lee & Shepard, 1974.
36. *Town Mouse Country Mouse* by Jan Brett. G. P. Putnam, 1994.
37. *Tuesday* by David Wiesner. Houghton, 1992.
38. *What's the Big Idea, Ben Franklin?* by Jean Fritz. Putnam & Grosset, 1976.
39. *Where the Sidewalk Ends* by Shel Silverstein. Harper & Row, 1974.
40. *Where the Wild Things Are* by Maurice Sendak. Harper & Row, 1964.

Fact or Fiction?

Purpose

To have students decide whether information is factual or fictional.

To have students play a game as a follow-up to stories with dragon characters.

To Make

Prepare a list of statements that either relate to words with "dragon" in them that are factual and statements pertaining to fictional books with dragon characters in them.

Examples of statements follow this page.

Make two copies of the sample dragon.

⏰ Preparation time—30 minutes

To Play

Read stories that have dragon characters.

Follow-up by discussing the terms fiction and fact.

Divide the class into two teams. Have each team decide on the scorer.

Give a copy of the dragon page to the scorer.

Start by reading a factual statement or a fiction statement to one member of a team and direct that student to respond by saying whether that statement contains factual or fictional information. If the response is correct, tell that team's scorer to shade in one of the plates on the back.

Continue with the other team. The winning team is the one with the largest number of shaded plates.

Dragon Stories

A Friend for Dragon by Dav Pilkey. Orchard, 1991. A dragon is frustrated in his attempts to befriend an apple.

Komodo! by Peter Sis. Greenwillow, 1993. A boy travels to the island of Komodo to see the dragons.

The Popcorn Dragon by Jane Thayer. Morrow Junior, 1989. Dexter's friends decide his hot breath is not so bad after all when it pops corn.

Raising Dragons by Jerdine Nolan. Harcourt Brace, 1998. A little girl finds satisfaction in raising dragons —just like her father does in farming.

Fact or Fiction?

1. Fire-breathing dragons caused volcanoes to erupt. (fiction)

2. Dragons in China did good deeds and brought good luck. (fiction)

3. The dragonfly is a water insect with four large wings and compound eyes. (fact)

4. The Komodo dragon has sharp teeth and claws. (fact)

5. The Komodo dragon is related to the ancient dragons of Asia. (fiction)

6. Dragonflies help people by feeding on harmful insects like mosquitoes. (fact)

7. The snapdragon plants have beautiful flowers and many different colors. (fact)

8. Long ago a witch turned the snapdragon into a plant for "snapping" at her. (fiction)

9. Dragons were hunted by "knights in shining armor" to protect kings. (fiction)

10. The dragonfly's long body is either green, blue, or brown. (fact)

11. The flower of a snapdragon looks like an animal's head with lips. (fact)

12. Dragons, like the dinosaurs, became extinct. (fiction)

13. In The Popcorn Dragon, Dexter's liked him more when he used his hot breath to pop corn instead of showing off his smoky rings. (fiction)

14. Sea dragons could swallow ships in one gulp. (fiction)

15. Komodo dragons live on the island of Komodo and on other small islands in Indonesia. (fact)

16. A dragonfly uses its legs to perch, not walk, and to capture insects. (fact)

17. Dragon is happy at the end of A Friend for Dragon because he ends up with lots more friends. (fiction)

18. A little girl didn't get any help from her parents when she tried to raise her dragon in Raising Dragons. (fiction)

19. The Komodo dragon is the largest living lizard. It has a long tail and skin covered with scales. (fact)

20. Long ago the sky was full of flying green dragons. (fiction)

Fact or Fiction Dragon

Biblio - Baseball

Purpose

To review features of a nonfiction book.

To Make

Make two copies of the next page on card stock. Cut out and put the cards in a stack.

Draw a diamond shape on a chalkboard or dry-erase board and label it as shown in the example.

⏰ Preparation time—30 minutes

To Play

Get two nonfiction books that have an index, a glossary, a table of contents, and a bibliography.

Divide the class into two teams. Direct one student to stand at the board to mark the moves around the bases and to keep score. Tell the class how long the game will be played.

Have the first player on one team draw a card and respond according to the direction on the card. If the response is correct, direct the scorekeeper to put an X by the first base. If incorrect, the scorer puts "1 Out" on the board.

The game continues like baseball with a point for each player who reaches Home. When a player draws a "Fouled Out" card, the player does not answer a question, and the team receives an "out." After three outs, the other team go to bat.

The team with the most points at the designated time limit wins the game.

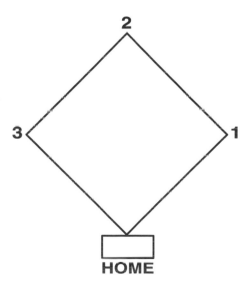

Bio – Baseball Cards

Locate the title.

Locate the author's name.

Locate the glossary.

Locate the publisher's name.

FOULED OUT!

Locate the title page.

Locate the table of contents.

FOULED OUT!

Locate the call number.

Show where book belongs on shelf.

Locate the illustrator's name.

Locate the index page.

Fly ball caught by the right fielder. OUT!

Locate the copyright date.

Fly ball caught by the left fielder. OUT!

Locate a bibliography on the topic.

Dewey Draw

Purpose

To familiarize students with the numbers of the Dewey Decimal Classification System and related subjects.

To Make

Prepare a set of ten cards on which are printed the words:

Draw 1 (make three)
Draw 2 (make three)
Draw 3 (make two)
Draw 4 (make two)

Then prepare a set of about 52 cards, each printed with a call number and the appropriate subject. A sample list is on page 34. Prepare several "wild cards."

Prepare questions related to the Dewey Decimal Classification System. Example questions are on page 35.

⏰ Preparation time—40 minutes.

To Play

Divide the class into two or three teams. Each team needs to designate one person to hold the Dewey cards won by the team. The card keepers need to form the team's cards into sets made up of four cards with the same first number (i.e., 568; 551; 599; 510). A wild card may be used to complete a set.

Shuffle both the "Draw" cards and the Dewey number cards. Keep cards face down and in separate stacks.

Start the game by asking a player from one team a question from your prepared list. If the player responds with the correct answer, have that player take a card from the "Draw" stack. Let that player draw the number of cards from the other stack indicated by the number on the "Draw" card. The player gives the card(s) to the team member responsible for keeping the cards.

Continue the same procedure with the other teams. The game ends when all Dewey cards are gone. The "Draw" cards may be reshuffled and used again during the game.

The winner is the team with the most Dewey sets.

Sample Dewey Call Numbers for Dewey Draw Game

332.4	money	510	mathematics
347.9	government	523.2	space
355.8	armor	537	electricity
363.73	pollution	551.2	volcanoes
383	postal workers	551.5	weather
387.2	ships	568	dinosaurs
391	clothing	581	plants
394.2	holidays	597	sharks
395	etiquette	598.1	reptiles
398.2	folk tales	598.2	bears
608.7	inventions	728.8	castles
625.1	railroads	737.4	coin collecting
629.1	rockets	743	drawing
629.22	trucks	780	music
636.07	farm animals	793.7	riddles
641.5	cookbooks	793.8	magic
636	pets	794.6	bowling
629.28	bicycles	796.32	basketball
646	sewing	796.33	soccer
629.221	model cars	796.357	baseball

915.2	Japan	403	dictionary
940.54	World War II	438	German
943	Germany	448	French
952	Ancient Egypt	468	Spanish
972	Mexico	493	hieroglyphics
973.3	Revolutionary War	495.1	Chinese
973.7	Civil War	495.6	Japanese
979.4	California	496	African languages
979.8	Alaska		
996.9	Hawaii		

Dewey Draw Sample Nonfiction Questions

1. Where are the nonfiction books in the media center?

2. How many major sections are nonfiction books divided into?
   a. 5   b. 10   c. 15   (b)

3. Are Dewey Classification numbers used with fiction books?   (no)

4. Which of these subjects does not belong in the 900 section?
   a. Ancient Rome   b. Korean War   c. Sign Language   (c)

5. Which of these comes at the beginning of the nonfiction section?
   a. 568   b. 398.2   c. 811   (b)

6. Are books in the 500s found at the _____ of the nonfiction section?
   a. beginning   b. middle   c. end   (b)

7. Give two examples of books that are in the 500 or natural science section.

8. Give two examples of books that are in the 600 or applied science section.

9. Give two examples of books that are in the 700 or arts section.

10. Give an example of a book found in the 200 or religion section.

11. Give an example of a book found in the 300 or social science section.

12. Go to the shelf and find a poetry book in the 800 section.

13. Go to the shelf and find a language book in the 400 section.

14. Put these 500 call numbers in the proper order:
    551.4   532.2   595

15. Put these 398.2 call numbers in order:
    398.2 Gri   398.2 Mot   398.2 Bre

16. Where would you find books on the different states of the United States?
    a. 500 (natural science)   b. 800 (literature)   c.900 (travel)   (c)

17. Where would you find books about dinosaurs?
    a. 500 (natural science)   b. 600 (applied science)   c. (mythology)   (a)

18. Do reference books have nonfiction call numbers?   (yes)

Media Marathon

Purpose

To review the order, alphabetically or numerically, in which materials are shelved.

To review the location of materials on the shelves.

To Make

Prepare five sets of cards, each set relates to a different group of library skills.
Use 3" x 5" size index cards.

Set 1: Fiction. Write fiction call numbers on ten cards, one call number per card.

Set 2: Nonfiction. Write nonfiction call numbers on ten cards, one call number per card.

Set 3: Material Call Numbers. Write types of materials and their call number symbols (one call number per card; one term per card) on sixteen cards.

Call Number	Materials
B	Biography
000 - 999	Nonfiction
F	Fiction
E	Easy Fiction
Ref	Reference
SC	Story Collection
VR	Video Recording
CD	Compact Disk

Set 4: Biography. Write five biography call numbers on five cards, one call number per card. Write the five titles of biographies that match the call numbers, one title per card.

Set 5: Shelf Hunt. Write five call numbers on cards, one call number per card, for materials on the library's shelves. Select call numbers from various sections of the library. Make sure materials with those call numbers are on the shelf. You might want to have more than one set of call numbers so that each team can have unique items to find.

⏰ Preparation time—40 minutes

You will need a timer to play this game.

To Play

Divide the class into five teams. Tell students that each player will participate in one of the five competitions. If there are fewer than five players, adjust as needed.

The marathon consists of five tasks, each task must be completed before the next is started. The tasks are as follows:

Task 1: Put the ten fiction call numbers in alphabetical order.

Task 2: Put the ten nonfiction call numbers in numerical order.

Task 3: Match the eight call numbers with the appropriate type of material.

Task 4: Put biography call numbers with matching titles.

Task 5: Locate the items with those call numbers at the shelves. Bring the items to the teacher.

Put the five sets of cards at five different locations so that the cards will not get mixed up. Shuffle the cards in each set so the cards are not in order, and reshuffle after each round.

At the "start signal" (start the timer) a player from one team hurries to do Task 1. After that task is completed and checked by the teacher or student monitor, the next person on that same team does the second task. Each task may not begin until the previous task is correct. At the completion of Task 5, the timer is stopped and the team's time is noted. Each task is performed by a different team member. The team that finishes the five tasks in the shortest time wins the game.

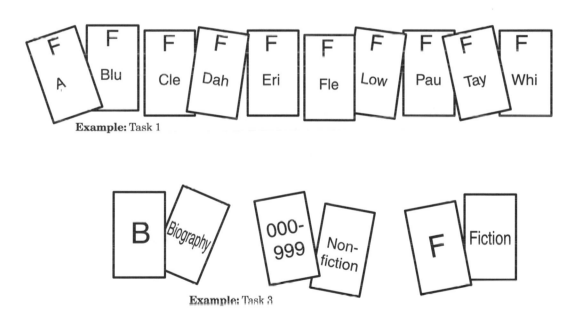

Example: Task 1

Example: Task 3

Media Puzzle

Purpose

To review general information related to the resources of the media center.

To Make

Copy the puzzle sheet on the following page, one for each student.

⏰ Preparation time—15 minutes

To Play

Divide the class into two or three teams. Give the worksheet to each student and allow them fifteen to twenty minutes to work on the answers with the other team members.

Play the game by having the teams take turns giving answers, one answer per turn. Each correct answer is worth a point. The team members can decide if each team member calls out an answer, or the team has a group spokesperson to call out all the team answers.

The team with the most points wins the game.

answer key

Learning about Books & Libraries

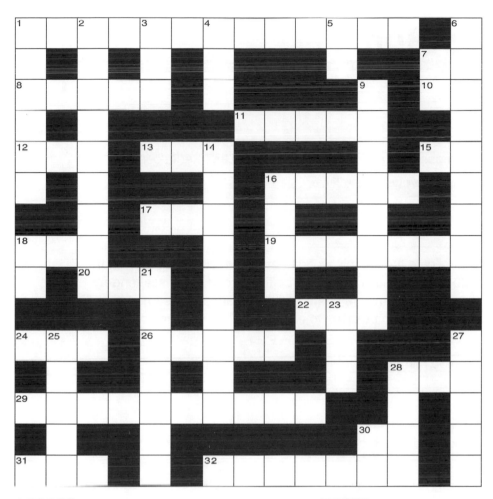

ACROSS

1. Author writes about himself/herself
7. Southeast (abbr.)
8. Name of the book
10. Call number for computer programs
11. Lengthy fiction book
12. _____ *Fine Day* (Caldecott winner)
13. Key to exit computer program
15. Call number for videocassette
16. Author of *The Lorax*
17. Key to erase on computer
18. Shiloh is this animal
19. Book has information on year's events; published once a year
20. Fairy-like creature
22. Allen _____, Caldecott winner
24. *The _____ Tree*, Caldecott winner
26. *Hero and the _____*, Newbery winner
28. What an atlas has
29. Book with factual information
30. _____ *Popper's Penguins*
31. Color of Clifford's fur
32. Name of award given to an outstanding author

DOWN

1. Person who writes a book
2. Illustrator's name may be found here
3. Grampa and others chase after this in Patricia Polacco's book, _____ *Tree*
4. _____ *Moon*, Caldecott winner
5. Personal computer (abbr.)
6. Encyclopedias found in this section
7. Call number for a book many stories
9. A partial dictionary
14. Award for outstanding illustrator
16. What is on the belly of a Seuss character
18. Arthur's sister (by Marc Brown)
21. Invented story; not true
23. Willy is this animal (Anthony Browne is the author)
25. Ball-shaped representation of Earth
27. Call number found here
28. She had a lamb
30. *Dear ____ Henshaw*, Newbery

Scavenger Hunt

Purpose

To review the location of various print and nonprint materials in the media center.

To have students work cooperatively in an activity.

To Make

Prepare a worksheet (or duplicate the sample worksheet on the following page) that lists items you want the students to find. If teams will be timed, one list of scavenger items can be used for all teams. If teams are searching the library at the same time, different biography and fiction books can be given to each team. Make a copy of the hunt list for each student.

⏰ Preparation time—15 to 30 minutes.

To Play

Review where items are located in the media center and the order in which they are placed on the shelves.

Divide the class into five teams of four to five students per team. Give each student the prepared sheet. Tell students that each team must find all the items on the list, and that they as a team may decide how they want to find and collect the materials (i.e., students work together, in pairs, or each student responsible for several items).

The students search the media center for the items. When the group has collected all the items, one member brings them to you for checking. If correct, designate which group is first, second, and third in the completion of the task.

Optional: Use of a timer to time each group's time to hunt the materials.

Use of markers at shelves so students may put items back on the shelves in the correct order.

Scavenger Hunt

1. A book about Abraham Lincoln

2. A book with a call number in the 500s

3. A poetry book (811)

4. A fiction book written by Beverly Cleary

5. An Easy fiction book with an animal character

6. A book in the story collection (SC) section

7. An atlas

8. A periodical

9. A nonbook material (i.e., CD-ROM)

10. Three books on plants listed in the computer library catalog

Call number	Title
1. _____	_____
2. _____	_____
3. _____	_____

Geo-Word

Purpose

To familiarize students with geographical terms.

To provide students with practice using the dictionary.

To Make

Prepare and give to the students a list of about twenty geography-related terms. Write each word on an index card, one word per card.

You will need five individual chalkboards, chalks, and erasers.

⏰ Preparation time—30 minutes

⏰ Approximate time for students to look up definitions—30 minutes

To Play

Divide the class into five teams. Have each team assign a recorder to write the team's answers on the chalkboard.

Tell the teams that they are responsible for looking up the definitions of the words on the list. Each student is responsible for the definitions of about four words.

Give each team recorder the chalk, chalkboard, and eraser.

Pick a card from the stack. Look at the word on that card but do not show the word to the class. Give no more than two-word clues that relate to the word.

The team collaborates to decide on one of the words on the list to be written by the recorder.

At the "Boards Up!" signal, the teacher shows the card and the teams show their answers. Each team that has the same word as the teacher gets a point. The team with the most points at the end of the game wins.

Sample Clues

Clues for some of the words from the list on page 43.

1. alpine – like Alps
2. arctic – North Pole
3. canyon – large gorge
4. coastal – seaside
5. cove – small bay
6. crater – volcano "mouth"
7. delta – river "mouth"
8. dune – sand hill
9. glacier – icy field
10. gully – small gulch
11. island – Hawaii
12. latitude – horizontal line
13. longitude – vertical line
14. marsh – swampy area
15. oasis – green spot
16. peninsula – Florida

Look up the definitions of these words:

1. alpine

2. arctic

3. canyon

4. coastal

5. cove

6. crater

7. delta

8. dune

9. glacier

10. gully

11. island

12. latitude

13. longitude

14. marsh

15. oasis

16. peninsula

17. plain

18. plateau

19. prairie

20. tundra

Globe Trotting

Purpose

To play a game related to the study on continents.

To Make

Write the numbers 1 through 7 and the names of the continents on 8½" X 11" tagboard, one number and one continent per card as shown. Laminate twice to make the boards durable.

Write questions related to the seven continents on index cards, one question per card. Number the cards to correspond with the continents the questions are about and stack them according to their numbers.

You will need two bean bags for this game.

⏰ Preparation time—40 minutes

To Play

Tape the cards on the floor in the pattern shown below. Add a tape line for students to stand behind when they pitch the bean bags. Use masking tape to tape cards on floor.

Divide the class into two teams. Tell the students that their team members must pitch the bean bags on the numbers in sequence, starting with number 1, continuing with number 2, and either ending with number 7 or returning to number 1. Only one pitch is allowed per turn. Teams alternate taking turns.

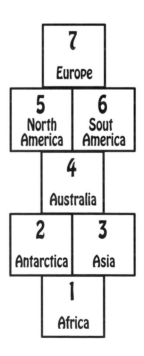

When the bean bag lands on the appropriate number, the team must answer a question related to that number (continent). If the response is correct, the team waits until the other team has its turn to follow the same procedures.

If the bean bag does not land on the appropriate card, the team loses its turn. If the team gives an incorrect answer, it must answer another question related to that number (continent) in order to move to the next number. The team that completes the 7 continents or returns to number 1 (optional) wins the game.

Authors' Note: Information about some countries may be found on Atlapedia Online Atlas (http://www.atlapedia.com/).

Questions about the Continents

Africa

1. Africa is the _____ continent (in land size)
   a. largest   b. 2nd largest   c. 3rd largest   (b)

2. Africa has 52 _____.
   a. countries   b. states   c. counties   (a)

3. Answer yes or no. Does the equator pass through Africa?   (yes)

4. Answer yes or no. Africa has the largest number of people in the world.   (no)

5. The Sahara is a   a. river   b. mountain   c. desert   (c)

6. Which ocean does not touch Africa?
   a. Indian Ocean   b. Atlantic Ocean   c. Pacific Ocean   (c)

7. Where would you most likely find these African animals: lion, antelope, zebra, giraffe?
   a. desert   b. grassland   c. tropical forest   (b)

8. In what country of Africa are the great pyramids found?
   a. Egypt   b. Kenya   c. South Africa   (a)

9. True or false? Almost all of the world's supply of diamonds are mined in Africa. (true)

Antarctica

1. Antarctica is the continent surrounding what pole?   (south)

2. True or false? The three largest oceans of the world touch Antarctica.   (true)

3. True of false? Antarctica is the smallest continent.   (false)

4. Would you find tropical animals in Antarctica?   (no)

5. Name two animals that live in Antarctica.

6. True or false? Antarctica is the coldest continent.   (true)

7. Which of these would not be found in Antarctica.
   a. glacier   b. jungle   c. icecap   (b)

8. True or false? The capital of Antarctica is Iceland.   (false)

9. True or false? It is too cold for animals to live in the waters surrounding Antarctica.   (false)

Asia

1. True or false? Asia is the largest continent in size and population.   (true)

2. Name a country in Asia.

3. Name two languages spoken in Asia.

4. Name an ocean that touches Asia.   (Indian Ocean; Pacific Ocean)

5. Tokyo is the capital city of what Asian country?   (Japan)

6. What is the only man-made structure on earth that can be seen by astronauts in space? This is located in Asia.   (Great Wall of China)

7. True or false? The highest mountain in the world, Mount Everest, is located in Asia.   (true)

8. Asia leads the world in the growing of what crop?   (rice)

9. Name a country in Asia that is an island country.   (Japan, Philippines, etc.)

Australia

1. True or false? Australia is the only continent that is also a country.   (true)
2. True or false? Australia is the smallest continent in land size.   (true)
3. Does the equator pass through Australia?   (no)
4. What language do Australians speak?   (English)
5. What ocean besides the Pacific Ocean borders Australia?   (Indian)
6. Name an animal unique to Australia.   (kangaroo; platypus; emu)
7. Which is the capital city of Australia?   a. Tokyo   b. Canberra   c. Saigon   (b)
8. What area is located in Australia?
   a. Death Valley   b. The Gobi Desert   c. The Outback   (c)

North America

1. Besides the United States, name a country in North America. (Canada; Mexico)
2. True of false. The continent of North America is larger than Africa.   (false)
3. Name a major river in North America.   (Mississippi; Ohio; Missouri)
4. Does the equator pass through North America?   (no)
5. What country separates 48 U.S. states from the 49th U.S. state?   (Canada)
6. Name a mountain range in North America.   (Rocky Mts.; Appalachian Mts.)
7. What language, other than English, is spoken in North America? (Spanish;French)
8. Is Canada divided into states?   (no, provinces)
9. How many lakes make up the Great Lakes?   (5)

South America

1. Do all the people from South America speak the same language?   (no)
2. Does the equator pass through South America?   (yes)
3. Name an ocean that touches South America.   (Pacific; Atlantic)
4. Which river is located in South America?   a. Amazon   b. Nile   c. Colorado (a)
5. Are Brazil, Chile, and Peru located in South America?   (yes)
6. Which mountains are located in South America?
   a. Alps   b. Andes   c. Himalayas   (b)
7. True or false? South America is larger in land size than North America.   (false)
8. True or false? Bananas, cocoa, sugar, and cotton are big exports to North America. (true)

Europe

1. Name a country in Europe.
2. Name a capital city in Europe.
3. True or false? Europe is the smallest continent.   (false)
4. Does the equator pass through Europe?   (no)
5. Do all people in Europe speak the same language.   (no)
6. Which mountain range is found in Europe?   a. Alps   b. Appalachian   c. Andes   (a)
7. True or false? Europe has the largest population in the world.   (false)
8. Where do more people live—Europe or North America?   (Europe)

Continent Conquest

Purpose

To play a game related to the study of continents.

To Make

Laminate a world map (or one with just continents). Use a marker to mark the numbers 1 through 7 on each continent, one number per continent.

Prepare a set of questions related to the seven continents on index cards, one question per card. Sample questions are on pages 45–46, following the game "Globe Trotting."

Make four ships, one per team. See examples on the next page.

You will need an eight-sided die. The dice may be purchased from a school supply store. *Optional:* Make a spinner as shown in the example.

⏰ Preparation time—40 minutes

To Play

Place the question cards on the appropriate continents. Divide the class into four teams and designate each team's ship.

Direct one team to start the game by having a student from that team roll the eight-sided die or spin the spinner. Place the team's ship on the continent that matches the number rolled. The player then draws a question card for the continent. The player may be required to give the answer, or allowed to confer with the rest of the team. If the team or team player's answer is correct, the team may continue the same procedure with another player.

The team's turn ends when the team or team player's response is incorrect. The ship is considered "shipwrecked" and remains on the continent where the incorrect answer was given. Other teams follow the same procedures. The first team may get another turn if all the other teams' ships are "shipwrecked."

No team may move their ship to another continent until they answer correctly.

If a team rolls an eight, that team automatically loses a turn. Also a team may not revisit a continent. If the team rolls the number of a continent it has already visited, that team also loses a turn.

The game ends when one team completes visits to all the continents.

Continent Conquest Ships

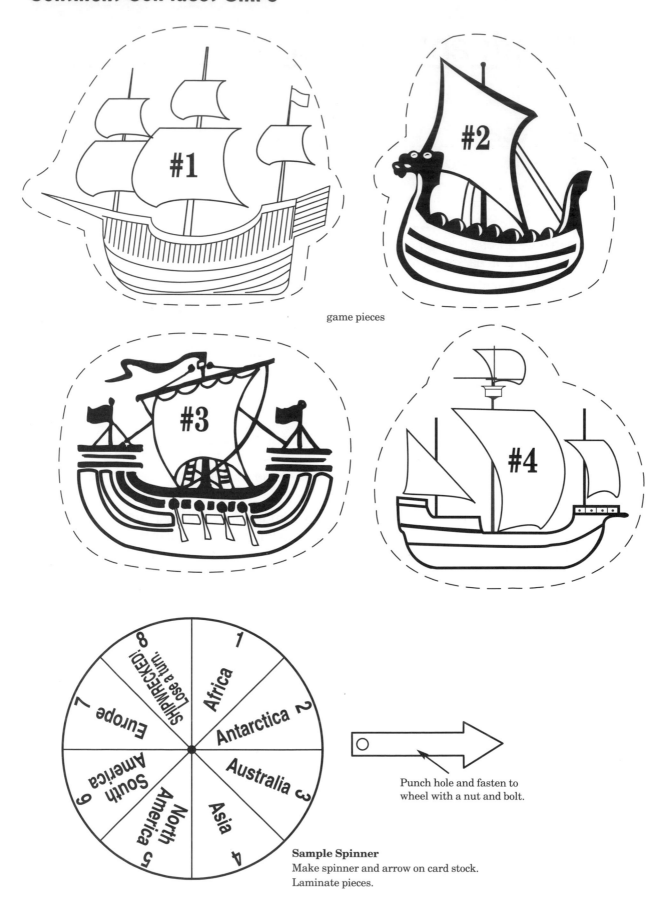

game pieces

#1

#2

#3

#4

Punch hole and fasten to
wheel with a nut and bolt.

Sample Spinner
Make spinner and arrow on card stock.
Laminate pieces.

1 Africa
2 Antarctica
3 Australia
4 Asia
5 North America
6 South America
7 Europe
8 SHIPWRECKED! Lose a turn.

Check Points

Purpose

To provide students with practice locating geographic information using an atlas, a globe, and computer resources.

To Make

Draw a 16" X 30" rectangle on a large sheet of wrapping paper or "butcher" paper. Draw lines 2" apart horizontally and vertically as shown in the example on the next page. Cut fifteen 1" magnetic strips (may be purchased at craft or school supply stores) to use as game pieces. There will be three teams, so select three colors and color five game pieces for each team.

Duplicate the worksheet on page 51 for each student.

⏰ Time to make the game—30 minutes

⏰ Time for students to do research for the game—30 minutes

⏰ Time to check the information—20 minutes

To Play

Divide the class into three teams. Direct the teams to compile as much information on the worksheets as they can in 30 minutes. Each team member needs to research three to four items, and each team needs a recorder to write the information on one master worksheet.

Check the information on the master worksheets. Teams will get one jump for each correct answer. Let each team know how many total moves they have earned.

Then mount the grid sheet on a magnetic board with magnets. Add the magnetic game pieces as shown in the example board on page 50. Designate one student to move all the pieces at the board and to tally how many times the teams move. The teams need to tell that person where they wish to have their game pieces moved.

The object of the game is to have the most game pieces in the Home area of the board when the game ends. Teams take turns moving forward or diagonally forward one square at a time (unless they are jumping another piece). No side moves or backward moves are allowed. Teams may jump their own pieces or the other teams' pieces. If a jump move is over another team's game piece, that piece is removed, as in Checkers.

Each team may only move the number times they earned in the research part of the game. If the number of correct responses is nineteen, that team may move nineteen times throughout the entire game. Although each team makes only one move per turn, as in Checkers, one move may include jumping over several game pieces.

The game ends when one team gets all its surviving pieces Home. But the winner is the team that has the most game pieces on the Home area when the game ends.

Check Points Game Board

Identify the following geographic locations:

Give specific examples for the items listed here, not definitions of the terms.

1. A river _____

2. An ocean that touches Asia _____

3. A mountain _____

4. A lake _____

5. A sea _____

6. An island _____

7. A desert _____

8. A gulf _____

9. A cape _____

10. A province of Canada _____

11. A capital in Europe _____

12. A country in the northern hemisphere

_____

13. A country in the southern hemisphere

_____

14. A country in Central America _____

15. A canal _____

16. A peninsula _____

17. A country in Asia _____

18. A mountain over 10,000 feet _____

19. A country in Africa _____

20. A country in the Middle East _____

21. A country in South America _____

22. A country the equator passes through

_____

23. A country in Scandinavia _____

24. A state the Rocky Mountains pass through

_____

Key Decisions

Purpose

To review the functions of selected keys on a computer keyboard.

To Make

Prepare questions related to the function of the keys. See the sample questions below. You will need individual chalkboards, erasers, and chalks, one of each for each team.

⏰ Preparation time—20 minutes

To Play

Divide the class into at least six teams. Give a chalk, chalkboard, and eraser to each team. Have the teams select a team recorder.

Read a question from the prepared list. Allow a few minutes for team members to confer on their answer. Direct the recorders not to show the answers until the "Boards Up!" command is given.

Call out "Boards Up!" All recorders must stop writing and show their boards. Give each team with the correct answer a point. Continue until all questions on the prepared list have been answered. The team with the most points wins the game.

Sample Questions for Key Decisions

1. What key do you use to erase a word?
2. What key do you use to get out of a program?
3. What key do you use to make spaces between words?
4. What key do you use to indent a paragraph?
5. What key do you use to get to the next line to start a new paragraph?
6. What key do you use to see more of the text or to get to the next page?
7. What key do you use to type all the words in capital letters?
8. What key do you use to type just one letter in capital letter?
9. What do you do to delete an entire file?
10. What do you do to safely shut down the computer?
11. What do you do to see more of the right side of the screen?
12. What do you do to see a previous page?
13. What do you do to print what you see on the screen?
14. What key do you use to go back a letter or words on the same line?
15. What do you do to type the $ instead of 4?
16. Give an example of a search engine.
17. Give an example of an icon.

Letter Keys

Purpose

To review the letter and punctuation keys on a keyboard.

To Make

Make two copies of the Keyboard Score Sheet (p. 54). Then cut 31, ¾" squares out of card stock and put the letters of the alphabet on them, one letter per square. Also make squares for the punctuation marks shown on the keyboard below.

⏰ Preparation time—30 minutes

make square using these letters and punctuation marks

To Play

Divide the class into two teams. Put the squares in a paper bag. Give a Keyboard Score Sheet to each team. Have the teams select their recorders.

Start the game by having one player reach into the bag and pull out a square. That player places the square on the appropriate spot on his/her team's keyboard score sheet. If correct, the team gets a point, and the recorders for both teams add the correct answer to the Keyboard Score Sheet. That square is then put aside, not in the bag. If the answer is not correct, the square is put back into the bag.

Continue the same procedure with the other team. The game ends when the bag is empty. The side with the most points wins the game.

Letter Keys Score Sheet

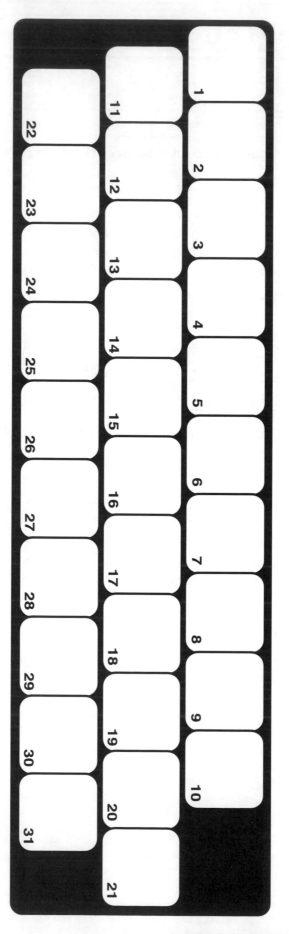

Net Challenge

Purpose

To have students explore various websites.

To have students keep card files of websites.

To Make

Make a list of at least ten websites that you want the students to explore. Prepare questions that relate to those sites. See the examples of websites and related questions on page 56.

⏰ Preparation time—30 minutes

⏰ Time for students to explore the websites—1 week

To Play

Divide the class into at least five groups. Give each student the list of websites. Direct teams to divide the responsibility for exploring the various websites. Have the students write on index cards the types of information the particular site has.

Allow a time for team members to explore the sites and to share the information with each other.

When the game is played, ask a member of one team a question. The other teams either agree with the answer or "challenge" the answer. In a challenge, the team being challenged must prove that their answer is correct by going to the computer and locating the information. If correct, the team gets one point for giving the right answer and another point for proving their answer was correct. The team making the unsuccessful challenge loses one point. If the team being challenged can't find the information to prove their answer was correct, they lose a point. If there is no challenge, it is assumed the team who answered the question is correct and they get a point.

Continue the same procedure with the other teams. When all the questions have been asked, the team with the most points wins the game.

Sample Websites for Net Challenge

Children's Literature Web Guide
http://www.ucalgary.ca/~dkbrown/index.html

Acme Pet - Animal Chat Rooms
http://www.acmepet.com/

Weathernet
http://cirrus.sprl.umich.edu/wxnet

Virtual Tourist
http://wings.buffalo.edu/world

City Net
http://www.City.net

Atlapedia Online Atlas
http://www.atlapedia.com/

Kid's Window to Japanese Culture
http://www.jwindow.net/KIDS/

The White House
http://www.whitehouse.gov

The Nine Planets
http://seds.org/nineplanets/nineplanets

Welcome to the Planets
http://pds.jpl.nasa.gov/planets

Volcano World
http://volcano.und.nodak.edu/

Field Museum of Natural History
http://www.fmnh.org

Which website would most likely have:

1. Today's weather
2. The list of Caldecott Medal winners
3. Kanji characters used in China and Japan
4. Hotels, with price information, in various cities
5. Map of a country
6. Information about U.S. presidents
7. Hurricane updates
8. Care of a cat
9. Current events
10. About food in Japan
11. Something to see in Chicago
12. *Voyager* discoveries on Saturn
13. Photographs of terrain on Mercury
14. Last volcanic eruption in Mexico

Biography Triple Match

Purpose

To review biography books.

To Make

Select eight books that are biographies. On separate index cards write the titles, the subjects (persons books are about), and their call numbers. There will be 24 cards in all.

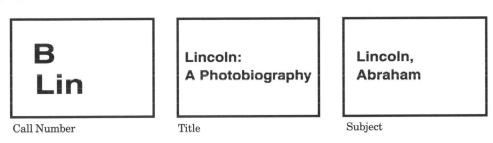

Call Number   Title   Subject

⏰ Preparation time—30 minutes

To Play

Place the 24 cards on a sentence chart board with the words face down. Give each student the opportunity to turn over three cards to make a three-way match: title, call number, and subject. If the cards match, give the student a bookmark or a slip of paper to be used for a drawing at a later date (once a month, special days, etc.). Possible prizes might include a paperback book or a special privilege.

Remove the matched cards and continue with other students. At some point you may want to put some cards back as the matches become too easy (six cards left on the board).

Biography Challenge

Purpose

To review biography call numbers.

To provide students with practice putting biography call numbers in order.

To Make

Duplicate five copies of page 59 on card stock. Cut the pages apart along the solid lines, putting the cards from each page in a separate envelope.

⏰ Preparation time—30 minutes

To Play

Review biography call numbers and shelving with students.

Divide the class into five teams. Give each team an envelope with the biography call numbers in it. Explain that in each "heat" or round, only two players from each team may participate.

At the "start" or "go" signal, the two members of each team work together to put all the call numbers in order. When they finish, they yell out "Done!" and put their hands up in the air.

The teacher determines who is first, second, third, and fourth to complete the task. If any team attempts to move any cards after they put their hands up, that team is disqualified.

Check the cards to see if they are in order. Those teams who have the correct order receive three points for first place, two points for second place, and one point for third place. The fourth-place winner does not get any points unless one of the three teams that finished faster does not have the correct order. In that case, the fourth-place winner moves up to third.

If any of the cards have been left in the envelope, that team is disqualified for having fewer cards than the other teams.

Continue this activity with several "heats" or rounds. Make sure that each team member has a chance to participate. Add up the scores and announce the team with the most points as the winner.

B **FRA** Benjamin Franklin	**B** **KIN** Martin Luther King Jr.	**B** **ROO** Eleanor Roosevelt
B **MIC** Michelangelo	**B** **TUB** Harriet Tubman	**B** **LIN** Abraham Lincoln
B **CAR** George Washington Carver	**B** **JOR** Michael Jordan	**B** **POC** Pocahontas
B **COL** Christopher Columbus	**B** **KEL** Helen Keller	**B** **BEE** Ludwig von Beethoven

Achievements

Purpose

To use with a review of the biography section.

To Make

Use the computer to make the numbers 1 through 25. Cut out the numbers and paste in numerical order around the edges of a poster board as shown in the example below. The numbers should be at least 1" high to be visible to the entire class.

Below each number, write one of the following letters: E, T, I or H (see sample board). The letters represent the four biography categories *Eureka!*; *Inventors*; *Tsk! Tsk!*; and *Honors* used in the game. Write the game title <u>Achievements</u> in the center of the board and paste four book pockets below the word. Write the categories on the book pockets, one per pocket.

Write questions related to the categories on 3" X 5" index cards. Several questions related to the same person can be on a single card. Examples of questions are provided on the next page. Place the cards in the appropriate pockets.

You will need a spinner or die to determine the number of moves and clothespins, clamps, or large clips to mark the moves on the board.

🕑 Preparation time—30 minutes.

To Play

Divide the class into two teams. Direct the first player to spin the spinner. Place the clothespin or clip at the appropriate spot on the poster board. Pull a card from the book pocket with the matching category. Read the question to that player.

If the player responds correctly, the marker is left on that space. If the response is incorrect, move the marker to the starting point. Follow the same procedure with the other team. The first team to reach the last number (25) wins the game.

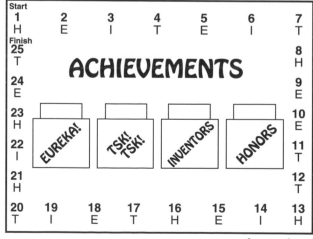

sample game board

Achievements Questions

Eureka!

1. "Eureka!" was the cry at John Sutter's mill. "Forty-niners" headed out West to stake claims. Where was his mill and what do we call this outpouring of fortune hunters? (California; Gold Rush)

2. Whose experiment with a kite during a thunderstorm proved that lightning is electrical? (Benjamin Franklin)

3. Sir Edmund Hillary and Tenzing Norgay were the first men to reach the peak of the world's highest mountain. What mountain was this? (Mt. Everest)

4. In 1928 Alexander Fleming discovered mold that dissolved germs. His discovery led to the production of a powerful germ killer used for treating infectious diseases. What do we call this medication? (penicillin)

5. Who was the first European to see the eastern shore of the Pacific Ocean? (Vasco Nunez de Balboa)

6. Richard E. Byrd made the first flight over these two areas. Name one of them. (North and South Poles)

Tsk! Tsk!

1. Benedict Arnold's name is equated with the word "traitor" for plotting to turn the fort at West Point over to the enemy. During what war did this happen? (Revolutionary War)

2. Although he brought many settlers to the Kentucky frontier, he died not owning any land in Kentucky. Who is he? (Daniel Boone)

3. What daughter of an American Indian chief never made it back to America after marrying an Englishman. She died of smallpox while waiting to sail back to her native land. (Pocahontas)

4. Susan B Anthony was among those women who led the Women's Suffrage Movement. What right was granted by the 19th Amendment to the Constitution, as the result of this movement? (women given the right to vote)

5. What infamous act did John Wilkes Booth do on the night of April 14, 1865? (assassinated Abraham Lincoln)

6. William Henry Seward's purchase of this land area was ridiculed by many, and the purchase was called "Seward's Folly" and "Seward's Ice Box." This land later proved to be invaluable to the United States. Where is this land? (Alaska)

Inventors

1. George Washington Carver created more than 300 products from this plant. What was the plant? (peanut)

2. He was known for his greatest invention, the electric light. He patented more than 1,100 inventions. Who was he? (Thomas Alva Edison)

3. George Washington is said to have asked her to make the first official "stars and stripes" flag of our country. Who is she? (Betsy Ross)

4. Kitty Hawk, North Carolina, was the site where this amazing vehicle was built and tested by two brothers. What was this famous creation? (Wright brother's airplane)

5. He was less known as an inventor than a diplomat. However, he did invent the glasses with the bifocal lens and a type of stove. Who is this famous American? (Benjamin Franklin)

6. Who started the concept of the assembly line to produce affordable products? His "horseless carriages" made by his factory were available to the less wealthy. (Henry Ford)

Honors

1. Despite her loss of sight and hearing, she became an inspiration to many because of her perseverance to be educated and her willingness to help those with similar disabilities. Who is she?   (Helen Keller)

2. Who guided more than 300 slaves to freedom?   (Harriet Tubman)

3. Who was honored with the Nobel Peace Prize and a national holiday because of his leadership in pressing for equal rights among our country's citizens. (Martin Luther King, Jr.)

4. Who was known as the "Angel of the Battlefield"? She founded the American Red Cross.   (Clara Barton)

5. Who was the first American to orbit the earth and who returned to space at age 77? (John Glenn)

6. Samuel Langhorne Clemens is one of the most popular authors of American literature. He told tales of Huck Finn and Tom Sawyer. What was his pen name? (Mark Twain)

Guess Who?

Purpose

To promote reading of biography books.

To play as a culminating activity during the reading of biographies.

To Make

Assign each student the task of reading a biography and reporting on the person to the entire class.

Write the name of the person each student reports about on large cards or 8" x 11" sheets of paper, one name per card or sheet.

⏰ Preparation time—one to two weeks for students to read a biography; several days for students to report on their subjects. Ten minutes to write the names on cards or paper.

To Play

Pin a card with a person's name on the back of each student. Make sure that the student does not get the name of the person about whom he/she gave a report.

Select a student to stand before the class and direct that person to turn around to show the class whose name is pinned on the card. Have the student turn to face the class and select up to three students to give information about the mystery name.

The student must then guess whose name is pinned on his/her back. Continue the same procedure with another student.

No scores are necessary for this game. The reward is for the student's individual satisfaction of guessing the right person. *Optional:* Divide the class into two teams and give a point for each person who can guess the right person after hearing the clues.

Doggy Romp

Purpose

To follow up stories with dog characters.

To Make

To make the game board, draw a doggy path using the example on page 65. Add a pond and a dog house as shown. Write "Stop for a drink. Lose a turn." beside the pond and HOME on the last block. Write START beside the first block.

Make two copies of page 66. Cut out one of the pictures of the bone, dog food, cat, leash, collar, and frog. Paste these on the board as shown in the sample board. Next to the frog, write "Stop to chase a frog. Lose a turn." Write the name of the game, Doggy Romp, somewhere on the board. Laminate the board.

Cut the remaining photocopied sheets (except the frog) along the lines to create game cards. Also reproduce and cut out the dog game pieces on page 67. Paste all the pictures on tag board and laminate. Tape double-stick tape to the backs of the dogs.

Prepare questions relating to stories with dog characters. See some sample questions we have prepared for the primary level (p. 67).

⏰ Preparation time—40 minutes

To Play

Read stories that have dog characters. Divide the class into two teams and give each a dog game piece. Shuffle the laminated game cards and place them face down on a desk.

Begin the game by asking a player on one team a question from the prepared list. If that player gives the correct answer, have that person draw a card from the stack of cards.

Move the dog according to the directions on the card. If a paw print card is drawn, move the piece that number of spaces. If a picture other than a paw print appears, move the dog to the matching picture on the board. If the dog has passed the picture, move the dog back to the picture.

There are two "lose a turn" spaces: the pond and the frog. The team loses a turn only if the dog lands on those spaces. Alternate taking turns between the two teams. If any team member gives a wrong answer, the team does not take a card from the deck. The first team to get to home wins the game.

Books with Dog Characters

Angus and the Cat by Marjorie Flack. Farrar, Strauss & Giroux, 1959. Angus decides that having a cat around is better than being lonely.

Angus and the Ducks by Marjorie Flack. Farrar, Strauss & Giroux, 1957. Angus scares some ducks away though not too long.

Clifford the Big Red Dog by Norman Bridwell . Scholastic, 1985. This, and other Clifford books, feature a gigantic, red dog who either does heroic acts or innocently causes accidents.

Dog Breath by Dav Pilkey. Scholastic, 1994. Just when Hally Tosis's family can no longer tolerate his horrible breath, he uses it to bungle a burglary.

Goggles by Ezra Jack Keats. Macmillan, 1969 Peter's dog Willie snatches the goggles away from "big kids" who insist on taking the goggles Peter and his friend just found. Read also *Whistle for Willie* (Viking, 1964).

The Hallo-wiener by Dav Pilkey. Scholastic, 1995. Oscar's dog friends changed his nickname from "Wiener Dog" to "Hero Sandwich" the Halloween night his costume helped rescue them.

Harry by the Sea by Gene Zion. Harper & Row, 1965. Harry wreaks havoc at the beach when a wave washes seaweed over him and leaves him looking like a sea monster.

Harry the Dirty Dog by Gene Zion. Harper & Row, 1956. Harry retrieves the scrub brush that he had hidden when he gets so dirty that his family can't recognize him. Read also *No Roses for Harry* (Harper & Row, 1958).

McDuff Moves In by Rosemary Wells. Scholastic, 1997. McDuff finds a happy family who feeds him vanilla rice pudding and sausage. Read also *McDuff and the Baby* and *McDuff Comes Home*.

Where's Spot by Eric Hill. Putnam, 1980. Lift-the-flap book is especially fun for young children. Other Spot stories also available.

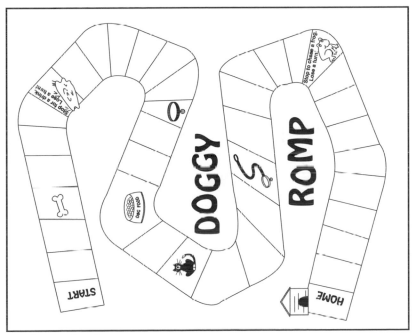

sample game board

Doggy Romp Cards

Doggy Romp Questions for Primary Grades

1. What dog is owned by Emily Elizabeth?   (Clifford)
2. What did Harry bury in the yard only to dig up later.   (scrub brush)
3. What dog loves vanilla rice pudding and sausages?   (McDuff)
4. What lived outside that Angus was most curious about?   (ducks/ cats)
5. When did Oscar dress up as a giant hot-dog bun?   (Halloween)
6. What was Hally Tosis's problem?   (bad breath)
7. Who hid from Angus for three days?   (cat)
8. Tell about one good deed done by Clifford.
9. What is the name of Peter's dog?   (Willie)
10. Why were people on the beach scared of Harry?   (looked like monster)
11. What dog's new home is at 7 Elm Road?   (McDuff)
12. Spell Spot's name.
13. Why didn't Harry like the sweater Grandma made him?   (had rose pattern)
14. In *Where's Spot*, was Spot hiding in the bathroom?   (no)
15. Where does Clifford take a bath?   (swimming pool)
16. McDuff got lost because he took off after what animal?   (rabbit)
17. Dav Pilkey wrote *Dog Breath* and *The Hallo-wiener*. Because he is the writer, he is called the _____.   (author)
18. What kind of books are the stories of Clifford and McDuff?   (fiction)
19. Susan Jeffers did the pictures for the McDuff books. She is an _____ *[artist]*. (illustrator)
20. Point to to the title. (Hand a book to a student and have them point to the title.)

dog game pieces

Railroad Crossing

Purpose

To use with a unit on trains.

To Make

Duplicate about seven "Go" and seven "Stop and Wait" cards from page 69. Write 25 questions related to the railroad and trains on 4" X 6" index cards, one question per card. Sample questions are on page 70.

Stack the cards with a "Go" card first and a "Stop and Wait" card last. Place three to four question cards after the first "Go" card. Put a "Stop and Wait" card followed by a "Go" card after the question cards. Continue stacking the deck following this same procedure ending with the "Stop and Wait" card.

⏰ Preparation time— 40 minutes

To Play

Divide the class into two teams. Start the game by asking the first team the questions on the index cards. Each time the team's response is correct, give that card to the team. That card represents one point. If the response is incorrect, set the card aside but continue asking that team questions until a "Stop and Wait" card appears.

When the "Go" card appears, switch to the second team and follow the same procedure, continuing to ask questions until the "Stop and Wait" card appears. Keep alternating between teams in this manner.

The game ends with the final "Stop and Wait" card. Count the scores by the number of cards each team receives and declare the winner.

Sample Train Books

Big Book of Trains. DK Publishing, 1998. Book has large and small photographs of various types of trains. Limited text.

Bigmama's by Donald Crews. Greenwillow, 1991. Donald Crews's childhood memories of his train trip to Bigmama's home in Florida. He also wrote *Freight Train* and *Shortcut*, both related to trains.

Little Engine That Could by Watty Piper. Platt & Munk, 1961. Popular tale of an engine who was persistent in delivering a load of toys.

Train to Somewhere by Eve Bunting. Clarion, 1996. A homeless girl is taken with a group of fourteen children from New York to the Midwest to be adopted in 1878.

Train by John Coiley. Knopf, 1992. Information on the history of trains, the future of trains, and "record breakers."

Sample Questions Related to Trains

1. Which train would a sleeper car belong to?
   a. freight   b. passenger   c. tender   (b)

2. What vehicle pulls the train?   (locomotive)

3. Name two types of cars that may be part of a freight train.
   (tank car, hopper car, box car, gondola)

4. True or false? Some atlases may have railroad routes?   (true)

5. True or false? A hopper car is used to carry automobiles.   (false)

6. What car is sometimes behind the locomotive to carry fuel for fire and spare water?
   a. cowcatcher   b. box car   c. tender   (c)

7. Early trains were sometimes nicknamed
   a. iron horse   b. stage coach   c. prairie schooner   (a)

8. True or false? Locomotives only pull freight trains.   (false)

9. A coach, lounge car, and dining car are part of what kind of train?
   (passenger)

10. Where is the cowcatcher located on a train?   (in front)

11. Name something that a hopper may be used to carry.
    (coal, grain, sand, other minerals)

12. Name something that a tank car may be used to carry.
    (milk, oil, chemicals)

13. Describe a gondola car.   (flat bed)

14. Bullet trains are used to carry _____.   (passengers)

15. Who drives in the cab of the locomotive?
    a. brakeman   b. conductor   c. engineer   (c)

16. What are some of the products carried by freight trains?

17. True or false. Rails are made from wood.   (false, they are made from steel)

18. What is the purpose of the coupler?
    a. to link the trains together
    b. to operate the railroad crossing lights
    c. to open the door of the train   (a)

19. True or false? Some cars need to have temperature controls.   (true)

20. What famous folk hero worked on the railroad?   (John Henry)

21. Who won the race between the iron horse named Tom Thumb
    and a real horse?   (the real horse)

22. Besides the conductor and the engineer, what other jobs are
    necessary to run a railroad company?

23. What was used to operate the first trains?
    a. electricity   b. solar energy   c. steam   (c)

24. Is *Train to Somewhere* a fiction or nonfiction book?   (fiction)

25. Locate an information source on trains.

Pig, Pig

Purpose

A game to use as a follow-up activity to a story with a pig character.

To Make

No preparation necessary.

To Play

Select five students to stand in front of the class. Direct them to put their hands over their eyes and try to guess who is grunting like a pig. Designate several students to grunt.

Each student at the front of the class has one chance to state who is the "grunting pig." If any of the students correctly identify any of the grunters, he/she gets to sit down and be replaced by the person(s) caught.

Continue this activity for several times.

Pig Stories

Cook-A-Doodle-Doo! by Janet and Susan Stevens Crummel. Harcourt Brace, 1999. Rooster gets help from a turtle, an iguana, and a pot-bellied pig as he tries to make Great-Granny's strawberry shortcake.

If You Give a Pig a Pancake by Laura Numeroff. HarperCollins, 1998. One problem leads to another if you give a pig a pancake.

A Perfect Pork Stew by Paul Brett Johnson. Orchard Books, 1998. Ivan tricks Baba Yaga into making a perfect pork stew without a pig.

Pig Pig Grows Up by David McPhail. E. P. Dutton, 1980. Pig Pig decides to grow up when he does a heroic, grown-up act.

Piggle Pie! by Margie Palatini. Clarion Books, 1995. Wolf relieves Gritch the Witch's frustration in her search for pigs for her piggie pie.

Pigs by Gail Gibbons. Holiday House, 1999. Colorfully illustrated primary-level book about pigs.

Pigsty by Mark Teague. Scholastic, 1992. Wendell can't clean up his room with the arrival of pigs.

True Story of the Three Little Pigs by Jon Scieszka. Dutton, 1995. Wolf's version of what really did happen when he went to borrow sugar from his pig neighbors.

Where's the Bacon?

Purpose

To play a game as a follow-up activity to stories with pig characters.

To Make

No preparation necessary.

To Play

Select one student to sit in a chair facing the wall. Direct the child to cover his/her eyes. Place an eraser under the chair.

Have the class sit in a semicircle. Select another student to "steal the bacon" (eraser). The student hides the eraser by sitting on it.

The class recites this rhyme:

> "Piggie, Piggie, where's the bacon?
>
> We've been looking. It's been taken!"

Explain that the student has three chances to find the culprit who stole the bacon. If that student successfully guesses the person, that student gets another turn. If not, the student who has the "bacon" gets to go up to be the next to look for the bacon.

Pig Pen-Up

Purpose

To follow up stories with pig characters.

To Make

Copy and enlarge the pig illustration below. Display it on the chalkboard for children to use as a model.

Prepare questions related to pigs or use the sample questions on page 74.

⏰ Preparation time— 20 minutes

To Play

Divide the class into two teams. Ask a player on one team a question related to pigs. If the student responds with the right answer, have that student draw a large circle for the pig's body. If the answer is wrong, the student sits down without drawing on the board.

Ask the other team a question from your list of questions. If the team player's response is correct, he/she gets to draw a circle for the team. The next question is directed to the first team. If the answer is correct, the team player draws a circle for the head on the team's pig.

The game continues with the teams taking turns answering questions. For each correct response, a player will add a pig part—the nose, eyes, mouth, ears, tail, or legs. To prolong the game and allow more students a turn, direct the teams to draw one eye, one ear, and one leg at a time. The first team to complete its pig wins the game.

pig illustration

Questions to Use with Pig Stories

1. What is a baby pig called?   (piglet)

2. Where is the snout of the pig?   (face)

3. What part of the pig is the nostril?
   a. hoof   b. snout   c. tail   (b)

4. How many toes on each foot does a pig have?   (4)

5. True or false? Pigs are the smartest of all farm animals.   (true)

6. Why does a pig wallow?   (to moisten skin, to keep cool)

7. Do pigs have good eyesight?   (no)

8. What is the snout used for?   (smelling, digging for food)

9. What do farmers feed pigs?   (corn, grains, table scraps)

10. Which is the weakest sense a pig has?
    a. seeing   b. smelling   c. hearing   (a)

11. What is the difference between a boar and a pig?
    (A boar is a male hog at any age. A pig is a hog usually less
    than ten weeks old.)

12. Which is the adult female hog?
    a. litter   b. swine   c. sow   (c)

13. Is a pig a mammal or reptile?   (mammal)

14. In what story is the pig character Wilbur?   (*Charlotte's Web*)

15. Name a meat that we get from hogs.
    (pork chops, ham, bacon, sausage, spare ribs)

16. True or false? Pigs do not have hair.   (false)

17. Tell a word that describes the sounds a pig makes.   (squeal, grunt)

18. A group of pigs a sow gives birth to at one time is called a
    a. litter   b. herd   c. flock   (a)

19. Does a pig have a long, short, or no tail?   (short)

20. A sty is a: a. sore spot on a pig   b. special food for a pig
    c. a pen for the pig   (c)

21. Which statement is incorrect:
    a. Pigs are nonliving animals.
    b. Pigs cannot fly.
    c. Pigs are pets to some people.   (a)

22. Is *Pig Pig Grows Up* a fiction or nonfiction book?   (fiction)

23. Is *Pigs* by Gail Gibbons a fiction or nonfiction book?   (nonfiction)

24. Is *The Three Little Pigs* a folktale?   (yes)

The Tortoise and the Hare Race

Purpose

To have students use a Venn diagram to organize information.

To Make

Sketch a path around the edge of a poster board. Write the numbers 1 through 25 as shown on the sample game board. Indicate start and finish lines. Make a copy of the four illustrations at the bottom of page 76 and add to the game board at the "x's". Add the name of the game to the center of the board. Duplicate the "Move Ahead" cards so there are at least sixteen in all (four of each) and cut apart. Stack face down.

Make a copy of the information sheet on rabbits, hares, turtles, and tortoises (p. 77) and two copies of the Venn diagram (p. 78) for each student.

You will need clothespins, clips, or clamps to mark moves around the board.

⏰ Preparation time—40 minutes

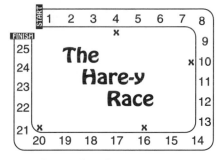

sample game board

To Play

After reading the fact sheet, have students label one Venn diagram page for turtle and tortoise information and the other for hare and rabbit facts. Allow time to complete.

Then divide the class into two teams; one will be the hares and the other the tortoises. Begin by asking a student to give a fact he/she has recorded and in what circle that information was written. If correct, have the student take a "Move Ahead" card from the stack. Mark the moves with the clothespin or clip. Continue with a player from the other team. If the marker lands on one of the picture spaces, follow the directions given there. The winner, not always the tortoise, is the first team to reach the finish line.

Tortoise and/or Hare Books

Guess How Much I Love You? by Sam McBratney. Candlewick, 1994. Bedtime chat between Little Nutbrown Hare and Big Nutbrown Hare on how much they love each other.

Rabbits and Hares by Emilie U. Lepthien. Children's Press, 1994. Simple information book with many colorful photographs about rabbits and hares.

Tops & Bottoms. Adapted by Janet Stevens. Harcourt Brace, 1995. By outwitting Lazy Bear, Hare manages to feed his hungry family.

The Tortoise and the Hare. Adapted by Janet Stevens. Holiday House, 1984. Delightfully illustrated book about the race between the hare and the tortoise.

What's Under the Shell? by D. M. Souza. Carolrhoda Books, 1992. Colorful photographs are on almost every page of this primary-level book about turtles and tortoises.

Rabbit and Tortoise Cards

Move Ahead **1**	**Move Ahead** **2**
Move Ahead **3**	**Move Ahead** **4**

Hare takes a nap under the tree.

Skip a turn!

Hare crosses a bridge and stops to admire his reflection.

Tortoise gets another move!

Lemonade 5¢

Hare stops for a cool drink of lemonade.

Tortoise gets another move!

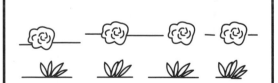

Hare sees a garden and stops to snack on carrots and cabbage.

Tortoise gets 2 more moves!

Rabbits and Hares

Rabbits and hares have good senses. They can hear the slightest sounds with their large ears. Their twitching noses easily pick up smells. Their eyes, located on the sides of their heads, see on both sides and behind. They cannot see directly in front of them.

Rabbits and hares are mammals with thick fur that keeps them warm when the weather is cold. They do not hibernate during the winter months. Their brown, gray, and sometimes white fur helps protect them by blending into their surroundings.

Most rabbits live in a den or burrow and prefer to live in an area with tall grasses or shrubs. These provide hiding places. Hares make their nests in open fields. Their longer hind legs help them escape quickly from their enemies. They thump their hind legs as a warning to other hares when a predator is nearby.

Hares are larger than rabbits. They have larger ears and longer legs.

A female rabbit is called a doe, and the male rabbit is called a buck. Baby rabbits are called kits or kittens. A female hare is called a jill, and a male hare is called a jack. The hare babies are called leverets.

Newborn rabbits cannot see or hear at birth and have no fur. Newborn hares are covered with fur, and their eyes are open.

Both rabbits and hares eat only plants (herbivorous). They have large, sharp, front teeth to rip up the grass and twigs. They go out looking for food from dusk to dawn. Hares go farther away from their nests to hunt for food. Rabbits remain close to their den or burrow.

Turtles and Tortoises

Tortoises are turtles that live on land. Tortoises are herbivorous. They eat plants and flowers. Turtles also eat plants. But many turtles eat fish, shellfish, snails, and insects. They can go long periods without eating or drinking water.

Tortoises move the slowest. They have thick legs and feet like those of elephants. Sea turtles have legs like flippers that help them swim quickly away from their predators. They can swim up to 20 miles and hour. Other turtles who live near water have webbed feet like the feet of ducks.

Turtles are reptiles. When the weather gets too cold or too hot, they burrow in sand or the mud near ponds, streams, or riverbanks. They bury their eggs in nests in the sand or dirt but do not guard their eggs. These unprotected eggs are not safe from hungry predators.

Not only does the number of turtles dwindle as predators eat the eggs, but people also catch turtles to eat or to make decorative items out of the shells. The slow-moving tortoises are in danger as they cross busy highways.

Venn Diagram

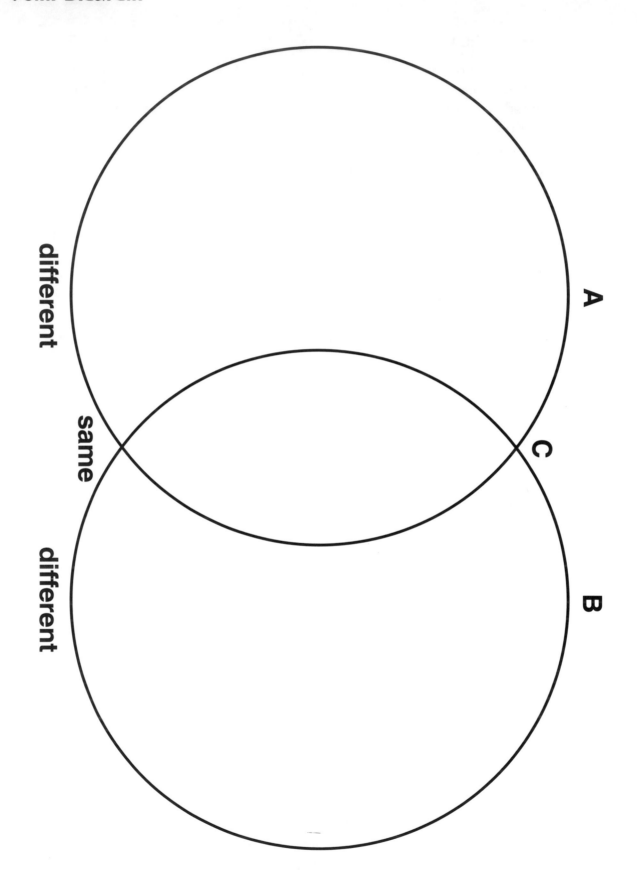

different

same

different

A

C

B

Friend

Purpose

To follow up a story that relates to friendship.

To Make

Purchase five ¾" or 1" wooden blocks from a craft store. Blocks cost about 19 cents each for the ¾" and 25 cents each for the 1". You may use five dice instead, and they may be purchased at a school supply store.

On the wooden blocks use a marker to write the letters F-R-I-E-N-D, one letter per side. On the dice cover the dots with stickers and write those letters, one letter per side.

You will need a cup for this game.

⏰ Preparation time—15 minutes

To Play

Divide the class into five teams. Tell each team that each member has one turn to throw the blocks or dice from the cup. Each team has a total of five "throws." As each team member takes a turn, record the score as follows:

If F appears (count just one F): 5 points

If F, R appear (count just one FR): 10 points

If F, R, I appear (count just one FRI): 15 points

If F, R, I, E appear (count for just one of each letter): 20 points

If F, R, I, E, N appear (same rule): 25 points

If F, R, I, E, N, D appear (Hooray!): 35 points

Total the scores from each team member's "throw." The team with the most points wins the game.

3/4" or 1" block

This shake worth 15 points for having F-R-I.

Love and Friendship Books

Charlie the Caterpillar by Dom De Luise. Simon & Schuster, 1990. Charlie chooses to be friends with a caterpillar who endures similar rejection from the other animals.

Corduroy by Don Freeman. Puffin, 1988. A stuffed bear searches for his lost button, so someone will buy him.

George and Martha by James Marshall. Houghton Mifflin, 1972. Many books on these two hippo friends are available. The books have very short chapters, cach a different episode and amusing.

The Giving Tree by Shel Silverstein. HarperCollins, 1964. This is a touching picture book about the sharing and sacrifice of a tree for the love of a boy.

I Love You Forever by Robert Munsch. Firefly, 1986. The love of a mother for her baby endures through the years as he becomes a man and she an old woman.

The Kissing Hand by Audrey Penn. Child & Family Press, 1993. A mother raccoon relieves her son's anxiety about going to school by giving him a secret—the kissing hand.

Guess How Much I Love You by Sam McBratney. Candlewick, 1994. Bedtime chat between Little Nutbrown Hare and Big Nutbrown Hare on how much they love each other.

Rainbow Fish by Marcus Pfister. North-South Books, 1992. Rainbow fish learns that selfishness leads to loneliness.

Voices in the Park by Anthony Browne. DK, 1998. Friendship develops between a girl and a boy in the park.

What Are Friends For? by Sally Grindley. Kingfisher, 1998. Sometimes a good friend like Jefferson Bear can get cross with his friend Figgy Twosocks despite all the fun playing and sharing.

Nihon – Go

Purpose

To have students play a game as a culminating activity during a study of Japan.

To Make

Copy and enlarge the kanji numbers on the next page. Cut and paste them around the edges of a poster board. Write the caption "Nihon -Go" in the center of the board. Nihon or Nippon is what the Japanese call Japan. Nihongo means Japanese.

Prepare questions related to your unit on Japan. Some sample questions are provided.

You will need clothespins, large clips, or clamps to mark the moves around the board and a spinner or die to determine the number of moves.

⏰ Preparation time—30 minutes.

To Play

Divide the class into two teams. Ask a person from one team a question from your prepared list. If the player responds correctly, have that person spin the spinner or throw the die. Move the marker the correct number of jumps. No moves are made if the response is incorrect. Start at (1). Continue the same procedure with the other team. The first team to reach number (25) wins the game.

Option: Japanese numbers are based on Chinese numbers. You may use this game board during a study of China also.

Sample Questions on Japan (primary level)

1. Japan's flag has a _____ sun.   a. yellow   b. red   c. orange   (b)
2. Japan is a _____.   a. country   b. state   c. city   (a)
3. Japan is an _____.   a. county   b. continent   c. island   (c)
4. What food is most important to Japan?   a. rice   b. bread   c. potato   (a)
5. What is the capital city of Japan?   a. Paris   b. London   c. Tokyo   (c)
6. What famous mountain is located in Japan?   a. Alps   b. Mt. Fuji   c. Rocky Mts.   (b)
7. Yes or No? The Chinese, Koreans, and Japanese speak the same language.   (no)
8. Japan is   a. smaller than the United States
              b. larger than the United States
              c. about the same size as the United States   (a)
9. The Japanese clothing is called   a. sari b.muumuu   c. kimono   (c)
10. The Japanese _____ when they greet each other.   a. bow   b. kiss   c. rub noses   (a)
11. Origami is the art of _____   a. pottery   b. self defense   c. folding paper   (c)
12. Besides rice, what other food is eaten a lot in Japan?   (sea food; soy beans; noodles)

Japanese Numbers

1 一	2 二	3 三	4 四
5 五	6 六	7 七	8 八
9 九	10 十	11 十一	12 十二
13 十三	14 十四	15 十五	16 十六
17 十七	18 十八	19 十九	20 二十
21 二十一	22 二十二	23 二十三	24 二十四
25 二十五			

Learning about Books & Libraries

BINGO (Japan)

Purpose

To play a game an an activity during the study of Japan.

To Make

Duplicate copies of the blank Bingo sheet and the picture squares for each student and 1 set for the teacher. Have the students cut out the picture squares. Cut the extra set of pictures to call the items.

Explain what each picture means. Some of the picture items are explained below.

You will need dried beans or card-stock squares for the students to use as markers.

☎ Preparation time—15 minutes

To Play

Direct the students to select nine pictures to place on their boards. Explain that once the first item is called, they are not permitted to rearrange their pictures. They may do so between games.

A student announces "Bingo" when his/her board has 3 items called in a straight line, horizontally, vertically, or diagonally.

Check the student's board. If correct, begin a new game. Students may rearrange their boards at this time.

Explanation of Bingo Pictures

kokeshi doll: popular wooden doll with no arms and feet

sushi: rice flavored with vinegar, sugar, and salt—sometimes served with raw fish

good luck cat: kept in stores to welcome customers and to wish for prosperity.

carp kite: flown during Children's Day (May 5); symbol of endurance and courage

geta: wooden shoes

origami: art of folding paper; wish for long life with 1,000 paper cranes

Tokyo: capital city of Japan

tabi: socks to be worn with geta or another type of shoes called zori

futon: thick quilt or comforter traditionally used for sleeping on floor

kimono: Japanese clothing

rice: "sticky" white rice served in a rice bowl eaten daily

1, 2, 3: Japanese numbers are written exactly like Chinese numbers

Mt. Fuji: at 12,388 ft. high, the highest mountain in Japan

flag: red sun for the country nicknamed the "land of the rising sun

Bingo Pictures

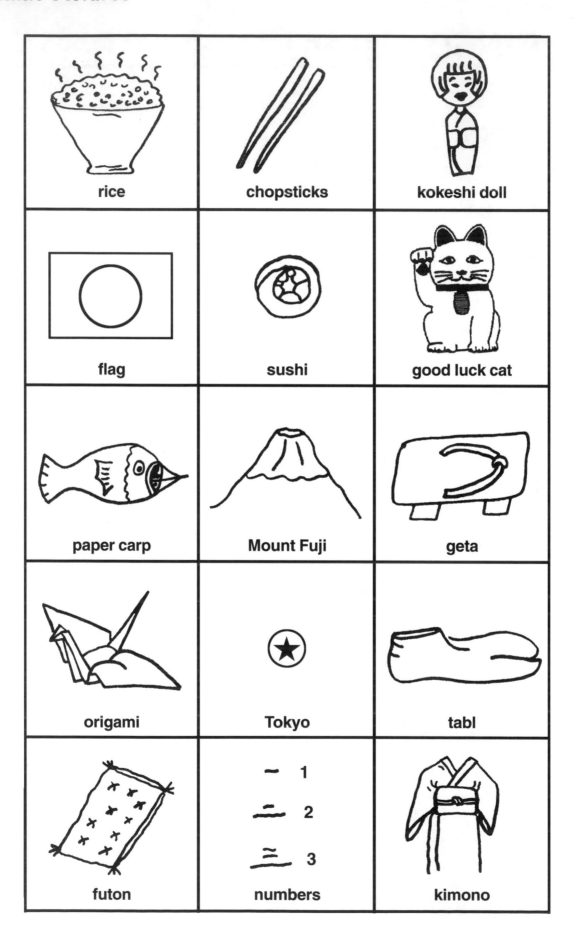

rice	chopsticks	kokeshi doll
flag	sushi	good luck cat
paper carp	Mount Fuji	geta
origami	Tokyo	tabl
futon	numbers	kimono

My Ship Has Come in from Japan

Purpose

Follow up to *Count Your Way Through Japan* by Jim Haskins (Carolrhoda, 1987).

The numbers one through ten are written in Japanese with their pronunciations. Illustrations of Japanese scenes, clothing, and objects accompany the numbers.

To Make

No preparation necessary.

To Play

Read the book Count Your Way Through Japan. Select one student to say, "My ship has come in from Japan."

Have the class reply, "What has it brought?" The student answers, " One _____ " (one item from Japan)

Continue with another student.

The student answers, " Two _____." (item from Japan)

The game ends when all students have had the opportunity to respond.

"Show Me!" (Billy Goats Gruff)

Purpose

To review various versions of the "Three Billy Goats Gruff."

To Make

Draw a grid, as shown in the example, on the chalkboard for each of the five teams.

Prepare questions related to the story. Some sample questions for kindergarten students follow page 87.

Team 1	Team 2	Team 3	Team 4	Team 5

You will need five individual chalkboards, five pieces of chalk, and five erasers.

⏰ Preparation time—30 minutes

To Play

Divide the class into five teams and give each team a chalkboard, eraser, and chalk. Tell the students that the team members will take turns recording the answers on the chalk board, each member recording two answers.

Read a question. Have the team members confer on the answer. The recorder writes the team answer on the board. Count slowly to twenty and say, "Show me!" The team recorders are directed to lift their boards. No more changes are allowed on the boards at this point.

Record the points (for each team with the correct answer) on the grid. Continue until all the questions have been asked. The team with the most points wins the game.

Three Billy Goats Gruff Stories

The Rough Gruff Goat Brothers by Bernice Chardict. Scholastic, 1995. Children will delight in this catchy rap version of the "Three Billy Goats Gruff."

Three Billy Goats Gruff by Ted DeWan. Scholastic, 1994. Captivating pictures abound in this modern version of an old favorite.

Three Billy Goats Gruff by Glen Rounds. Holiday House, 1993. This version has repetitive language that invites children to read along.

Three Billy Goats Gruff by Jim Lawrence. Modern Publishing, 1987. Large pictures and rhythmic words make this book especially appealing to children.

Three Billy Goats Gruff by Paul Galdone. Clarion, 1973. Simple text and sketchy illustrations are found in this version.

Three Cool Kids by Rebecca Emberley. Little, Brown, 1995. Street-wise goats meet a threatening rodent instead of a troll.

Sample Questions for the Three Billy Goats Gruff
(Kindergarten level)

1. The troll wanted to
   a. help the goats get to the hillside
   b. share his food with the goats
   c. eat the goats   (c)

2. The troll was the goats'
   a. enemy   b. friend   c. relative   (a)

3. Where did the troll live?
   a. near the bridge
   b. on the bridge
   c. under the bridge   (c)

4. The goats wanted to go to the hillside because
   a. they were looking for their mother
   b. the grass is greener there
   c. they wanted to see the troll   (b)

5. How did the goats get to the green hillside?
   a. swam   b. stepped on the rocks   c. crossed the bridge   (c)

6. The bridge went
   a. trip, trap, trip, trap
   b. clip, clop, clip, clop
   c. heave, ho, heave, ho   (a)

7. Write T for true and F for false. All the Billy Goats were frightened
   of the troll.   (F)

8. What did the third Billy Goat Gruff use to fight the troll?
   a. his horns   b. his hooves   c. his tail   (a)

9. The troll landed
   a. in the river   b. in the sticker bushes   c. on the grassy hillside   (a)

10. The third Billy Goat Gruff was the
    a. smallest   b. medium size   c. largest   (c)

11. The first Billy Goat Gruff said he was
    a. too small   b. too fat   c. too scared   (a)

12. Write T for true and F for false. The Three Billy Goats Gruff is a folktale. (T)

Where's My Momma?

Purpose

To help students understand that many animals find their mothers by their smell.

To Make

Saturate about twenty-four cotton balls with twelve scents, each scent on two balls, to use with twenty-four students. Add one scent and two cotton balls for each two additional students. The following may be used for scents:

butter extract	pickle juice	anise oil	fruit juice
perfume	vinegar	liquid from oil jar	ginger spice
scented shampoo	almond extract	garlic powder	peppermint extract

Put each ball in a sandwich-sized, self-sealing plastic bag. Close tightly so the scent does not escape.

⏰ Preparation time— 20 minutes

To Play

Divide the class into two groups. Designate which group will be the animal baby group. The other group is the animal mother group. Give each student in the "baby" group a scent bag. Have the two groups divided, at opposite sides of the room. Give their "mothers" a scent bag.

When you say, "Where's my Momma?" everyone opens their bags and smells. The "mothers" and "babies" try to match the scents in their bags.

Books to Use

Are You My Mother? by P. D. Eastman. Beginner Books, 1960. A bird, separated from his mother, asks others, "Are you my mother?"

A Mother for Choco by Keiko Kasza. Putnam, 1992 A bird discovers a mother who loves and hugs, though not similar in appearance.

Oats and Wild Animals by Frank Asch. Holiday House, 1988. Friends cannot replace mother when evening comes.

Stellaluna by Janelle Cannon. Scholastic, 1993. A bat has to learn the ways of a bird when she takes up residence with a bird family.

Dot - to - Dot

Purpose

Follow up to *Ten Black Dots* by Donald Crews (Mulberry Paperback, 1968).

Practice with mathematics questions.

To Make

Make a larger version of the sample grid pattern below on poster board and laminate. Or the grid pattern may be drawn on the chalkboard. The grid has four dots across and five dots down.

Write mathematical questions or problems. Some sample mathematical problems and questions for primary-level students are provided on page 90.

⏰ Preparation time—30 minutes

To Play

Divide the class into three teams: A, B, and C. Start the game by asking a member from team A a question or problem. If the player gives the correct answer, he/she picks two dots to connect, vertically or horizontally, but not diagonally. Lines are drawn on the laminated board with a erasable marker.

Continue the same procedure with the other teams, alternating turns among the three teams. When a team joins the dots to close a box (i.e., complete a square), that team claims that closed box with the team letter.

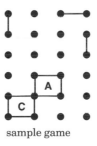

sample game

The team whose letter is in the most boxes wins the game.

sample grid pattern

Mathematical Questions for Grades K–1

1. How many days in a week?   (7)

2. How many days in a regular year?   (365)

3. How many months in a year?   (12)

4. How many legs does an insect have?   (6)

5. How many legs does a spider have?   (8)

6. How many legs does an ostrich have?   (2)

7. How many is a dozen eggs?   (12)

8. How many wheels on a tricycle?   (3)

9. How many fingers on a person? toes?   (10)

10. How many seconds in a minute?   (60)

11. How many minutes in an hour?   (60)

12. How many hours in a day?   (24)

13. What is the missing number?   5, 10, 15, 20, 25, 30, 35, _____.   (40)

14. What is the missing number?   10, 20, 30, 40, _____.   (50)

15. What is the number after 20?   (21)

16. What is the number before 20?   (19)

17. What is the missing number? 12, 13, 14, 15, 16, _____, 18   (17)

18. Add 1 + 1 + 1. What is the answer?   (3)

19. What is the missing number? 2, 4, 6, _____. 10   (8)

20. What is the answer? 9 - 6 = _____.   (3)

21. What is the missing number? 3, 6, _____.   (9)

22. Add 2 + 2 + 2 = _____.   (6)

23. How many days does September have? *(Look at the calendar.)*   (30)

24. How many legs does a ladybug have?   (6)

25. How many wings does a butterfly have?   (4)

Wodney Says

Purpose

To follow-up a story with a game.

To Make

No preparation necessary. You will need to read *Hooway for Wodney Wat* by Helen Lester. Houghton Mifflin, 1999. Rodney Rat overcomes ridicule and earns the respect of his classmates when he rids the class of its bully.

To Play

Read the book described above. Follow up by playing "Simon Says." Instead of saying "Simon Says," say "Wodney says...." . Start this game by having all the students stand. When you say "Wodney says," the students have to follow the command. If the command is given without those words, the students do not follow the command. If they do, they are directed to sit down. If you can, say the commands by substituting "r" sounds for "w." The object of the game is to have all students tricked into sitting down.

Backpack Race

Purpose

To follow up *My Backpack* by Eve Bunting. Boyds Mills Press, 1997. A boy's family discovers items missing after he gets a backpack from his grandmother.

To Make

Gather obvious and not-so-obvious items that a child might keep in a backpack and put them in two backpacks.

⏲ Preparation time—20 min.

To Play

Read the book *My Backpack.* Divide the class into two teams and line the students up into two lines. Put the backpacks on two chairs, each on a separate chair. At the "Go!" signal, have one student from each team run to a backpack and unpack the items in the bag. The next student from the same team runs to the bag and puts the items into the bag. The first team to have all team members either unpack or pack the team's backpack is the winner.

Honey Hunt

Purpose

To follow up a story related to bees.

To Make

Copy the honey pot (p. 93) on card stock. Cut out the picture and laminate it.

You will need a story related to bees. Recommended book: **The Bee Tree** by Patricia Polacco. Putnam & Grosset, 1993. Grampa, his granddaughter and others, chase after a bee as it makes a beeline to its hive.

⏰ Preparation time—30 minutes

To Play

After reading a story that relates to bees, select one student to leave the room. Hide the honey pot. Direct that student to search for the honey. The students will help by buzzing when the student is close to the honey pot. Have the students buzz louder the closer the student gets and softer as he/she moves away from the pot. When the student locates the honey pot, continue the same procedure with another student.

Following Rosie   Grade K

Purpose

To follow up the book *Rosie's Walk* by Pat Hutchins. Simon & Schuster, 1968. Rosie is totally unaware of who is following her as she takes a walk around the farm.

To Make

Prepare a course for students to walk through: a pond (towel on the floor); a haystack (small stack of books); the mill (teacher's desk); fence (chairs placed backward with space in between); and beehive (easel).

⏰ Preparation time—10 minutes

To Play

Read *Rosie's Walk*. Have students form a line. Lead them on the walk around the pond, over the haystack, past the mill, through the fence, and under the beehive. Give students candy corn at the end of the walk.

Grades K–1

Birds Can Fly

Purpose

To follow up a story with a bird or bat character.

Recommended book: **Stellaluna** by Janell Cannon (Scholastic, 1993). Stellaluna, a young fruit bat, settles in with a bird family when she becomes separated from her mother.

To Make

Write true and false statements as to which animals can fly.

For example:

1. Owls can fly
2. Penguins can fly
3. Bats can fly
4. Eagles can fly
5. Dolphins can fly

6. Ostrich can fly
7. Turkeys can fly
8. Frogs can fly
9. Ducks can fly
10. Robins can fly

⏰ Preparation time—20 minutes to write.

To Play

After reading a story that has a bird or bat character, have students stand up. Tell them to flap their arms if the statement is correct. If the statement is incorrect, they must stand still. The students who flap their arms when the statement is incorrect are directed to sit down.

Flap your arms and say the statements quickly so the students are "tricked" into flapping their arms even when statements are incorrect.

Learning about Books & Libraries